HOW VERY ENGLISH!

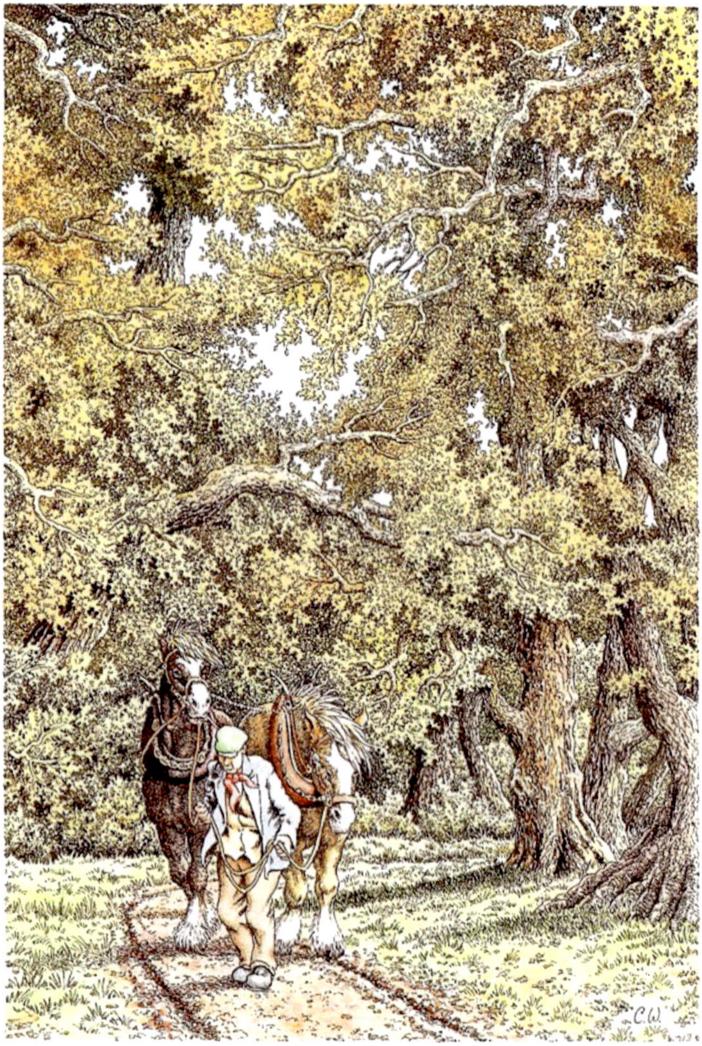
C.W.

HOW VERY ENGLISH

A Collection of Pastoral Poetry

By Colin Wright

(illustrated by the author)

Wildwood Publishing

First published in 2011 by:
Wildwood Publishing
4 Crown Green
Shorne
Gravesend
Kent DA12 3DT

© Copyright 2011
Colin Wright

The right of Colin Wright to be identified as the author of this work has been asserted by him in accordance with the Copyright, Designs and Patents Act 1988.

All Rights Reserved
No reproduction, copy or transmission of this publication may be made without written permission. No paragraph of this publication may be reproduced, copied or transmitted save with the written permission of the publisher or in accordance with the provisions of the Copyright Act 1956 (as amended).

ISBN: 978-0-9568547-0-4

Printed and bound in Great Britain by:
ProPrint, Remus House, Woodston, Peterborough PE2 9BF

CONTENTS

Part One – Reflections and recollections

Lost Highways	1
Corixa Floatata (The Unsinkable Boatman)	2
Remembering	3
The Henge	4
The Rut	5
The River	6
The Strike	7
Memories Of My Village	8
The Shingle Beach	10
A Cotswold Evening	11
How Very English	12
Glastonbury Abbey	14
The Shoreline	15
Symbiosis	16
The White Horse Of Uffington	19
The Wanderer	20
Something Sensed And Lost	22
The Sea Loch	23
The Stream Of Life	24
Night Storm	26
When Summer Never Came	27
The Pooh-Stick Regatta	28
The Endless Flow	29
Tintagel	30
Not Wisely, But Too Well	31
The Days Of Innocence And Dreams	32
Sunday Things	33
The Old Barn	35
Dawn Mist	37
The Galleon Moon	38
Innocence Recalled	39
The Kingfisher	40
Dancing In The Dark	41
The Dread Beast Of Night (a Gothic homage!)	43

Dawn And Fading Stars	44
Frinton	45
Night Glades	46
Pica Pica (The Magpie)	47
Two Greedy Owls	48
Gardening Break	51

Part Two – The Seasons

Spring At Last	55
Of Things To Come	56
Spring Blooms	57
Springtime In Seathwaite	59
Rebirth	60
Downland Hedgerows	62
Skiddaw Clouds, April	63
Late Spring, Evening	64
An Enchantment	66
Spring Magic	67
The Meadow Bank	68
A Village Morning, Summer	69
The Dragonfly	71
A House Martin Summer	72
The Lock	73
Interlude	74
The Sentinel	75
Sunlight On A Sycamore	76
Childhood's Last Summer	77
A Forest Spell	79
Summer Encounters	80
The Inland Sea	81
August Evening	82
Summer Sunset	85
A Summer Glade	86
The Harvest	87
Autumn Pastoral	88
Hiatus	90

The End Of Autumn	91
The Village In Autumn	92
Coming Home	94
The Stripper	95
The Team	97
Summergone	98
Autumn's End	99
Lamplight At Suppertime	100
Frosty Morning	101
In Wildwood Winter	102
Snow	104
A Cotswold Farmhouse Winter	105
Midwinter Night	106
Herdwick Ewes In February	108
Our Village – November 1917 (A childhood memory)	109
Old Winter	110
The Dreamer	111

List Of Illustrations

Frontispiece The Team

The White Horse Of Uffington	18
The Old Barn	34
The Dread Beast Of Night	42
Gardening Break	50
Springtime In Seathwaite	58
The Dragonfly	70
A Forest Spell	78
Summer Sunset	84
The Team	96

FOREWORD
(by Adam Holloway, Member of Parliament for Gravesham)

This is a beautiful collection of illustrated poems which captures scenes and nuances of quintessential England, together with a sense of vision.

The wonderful descriptions and imagery evoke a real impression of the places depicted and allow the reader to share them with the poet. The illustrations serve as a striking aid to the poems.

The days of long johns and royal banquets, simplicity and tranquillity, and much of traditional rural life may be long gone, but these poems ensure that the memory of such peaceful charm and beauty will last.

Great stuff

Adam

ABOUT THE AUTHOR

Colin Wright has been composing poetry for many years, and has been published in anthologies and magazines, and on the internet. He has illustrated several books, as well as supplying greeting card designs to major publishers.

'How Very English' his first collection, is the result of a desire to write poetry in an expressive, honest and accessible style reflecting a sincere affection for the countryside and rural life.

PART ONE

REFLECTIONS AND RECOLLECTIONS

LOST HIGHWAYS

Those wonderful canals:
The arteries of England till the swifter railways came,
Eclipsing with their smoking speed –
Those hustling, bustling iron-clad steeds –
Transport of a gentler, staider time.
The days of narrow-boats:
Brightly painted horse-drawn freighters
Ghosting through the ribbon waters,
Scorning hill and vale with hauteur –
Tiers of locks defying contour,
Mighty soaring aqueducts –
Once ferried what now goes by trucks.
All things mined and manufactured:
Steel from Sheffield,
Pots from Stafford,
Coal and grain
To Watford, Deptford.
All kinds of services and wares
From every source to everywhere
By waterways whose thoroughfares
Now largely lie in disrepair.

The packed earth tree-fringed towpaths
Hardened by ten thousand plodding hooves
Served highways in an age long gone,
Now byways just to ramble on.
Do they recall those horse-drawn days
When commerce travelled waterways
Through countryside that Constable
And Cotman thought might stay always?
Their great days may be past,
But how their peaceful charm and beauty lasts.

CORIXA FLOATATA (The unsinkable boatman)

The water boatman sculls and skims
The thin meniscus on the bright pool's rim.
He cannot sink, he is so light,
So boldly paddles round in sheer delight.
'I cannot sink, so cannot drown
And, therefore, paddle safely round and round!'

Two eyes watch closely from the reeds,
Gaze most intently as the insect speeds
And darts – this way and that – and then
Sculls heedlessly that way and this again.
The toad's tongue flicks out in a blink;
The boatman's sunk – though truly *didn't* sink.

REMEMBERING

The sweet sun-simmered smell of old, damp hay
Takes me drifting back to childhood years.
'Come Ned, come Nobbin, let's be on our way!'
Old Tom would call out, as he led the shires
At dawn up to the top field, where we'd play
Our games, encamped within the ruined byre.

And apple blossom's delicate bouquet
Promised endless spring on every breeze!
Each time I smell it now it's yestermay –
Those orchards with their ancient gnarly trees;
Tramping through them on our carefree way
To net tadpole and newts and water-fleas.

Later, when the laden orchards fruited,
We turned brazen outlaw, truth to tell.
Dauntless in our raiding, how we looted –
Apples, damsons, pears and plums as well;
Glutton-gorged ourselves till satiated
(though, if spotted, we could run like hell!)

Remember autumns up in Clay Lane woods –
Hazels crammed with juicy fat cobnuts?
Now they never seem to taste that good.
Is that just me, or simply growing up?
But, come to think of it, whatever could
Compare with childhood memory's brimming cup?

THE HENGE

A grey wind.
A whining single note conducted by the stones.
In stark surrounds is found
The dislocated circle,
Brooding, enigmatic and profound.
Bleak, dark, massive monoliths,
Weathered by millennia,
Like bones of ancient giants,
Earthbound.

THE RUT

A pale grey dew-drenched daylight stirs;
Dark ragged stands of lofty firs
Are silhouettes against the dawn.

Angry raucous bellows echo,
Ricochet from pine to pine.
Clouds of snorted breath-mist halo
Flung-back head and foam-flecked mouth,
The spring-steel arching spine.

Another strutting rutting challenge flung;
Accepted.

Dawn peace split by antler rattle,
Alpha and pretender battle,
Bone and muscle testing mettle
As the rivals lock and wrestle.

Unperturbed and unimpressed,
The hinds graze on
As if the outcome couldn't matter less.

THE RIVER

The satin-surfaced river mouth,
Quicksilver zest spent far upstream
In the heady rush of youth,
Now glides sedately, broad, serene.

But once it carved its way through cliffs
And plunged in cataracts and falls,
An eager torrent, brash and swift,
Which nothing in its path could stall.

Then, through the plains of middle age,
In sweeping curves meandering,
Its mood was calmer, stage by stage
More peaceful in its journeying.

Through water meadows fringed with sedge,
Where breeze-stirred graceful willows sway,
To rush-rimmed fens at delta's edge –
From source to shore it wound its way.

And now it murmurs of its past
And of the sea's embrace to come.
Its movements are now languorous –
It knows the course is almost run.

A milk-mist sky hangs over all –
A soft and creamy canopy.
A curlew tremulously calls –
A haunting, plaintive low 'coor-li'.

Then silence, broken only by
A gentle lapping on the hull,
The creaking of the oars I ply,
A distant, mournful mewling gull.

THE STRIKE

The patient, predatory heron waits among the reeds;
A statue, he, an obelisk, intent upon his heron deeds.
The silver dace dart cautiously, bright flashes in the stream.
They've never seen a heron, but they've heard a heron's victim scream.

'Best keep a watchful eye out, now,' one dace called to the rest,
'And pass the word around we're getting quite close to a heron's nest.'
Just then the patient heron struck like lightning from the shore.
The heron notched up one more strike. One dace would dice with death no more.

MEMORIES OF MY VILLAGE

Rising from their haze-blue drowsing shadows,
The stately slender poplars lined the lane,
An avenue of graceful swaying sentinels
At whose far end the village green was elegantly framed.

Nodding in the spring-warmed air like sages,
The poplars shed their cotton clouds of seeds
Like snowdrifts in the ditches by the lane sides,
Confetti-cascades strewn in wanton largesse by the breeze.

To either side the apple orchards blossomed;
Remembered fragranced days no years could fade.
How my head filled with that giddy perfume,
While sheep and plump geese quietly foraged in the pink-washed shade.

Sunday school was mostly well attended,
Though less for righteous reasons than for gain.
Regular attendance qualified one
For profitable carol singing when each Christmas came!

Cricket on the village green each Sunday.
Win or lose, the teams would try their best,
And break for buttered scones, cucumber sandwiches
And endless cups of tea then, fortified, play on with zest.

The manor house would host a fete in August,
Gymkhana, vegetable and flower show,
Aunt Sally stall, hoop-la and Punch and Judy,
And beer tent where each husband who could slip away would go.

One by one the young folk moved to town life,
As horse gave way to tractor, and machines
Replaced the old ways and the need for farmhands,
And life was changed for ever, and old England too, it seemed.

Often, now, I think back to my village,
Though years and circumstance have moved me on,
And, even though life brings rewards and riches,
Was life not truly rich enough in days now so long gone?

THE SHINGLE BEACH

The moon's white image fractured on the restless surface of the sea
and glistened on the tide-line bladder wrack and scattered shells.
Wind-tossed seabirds flashed like paper scraps against the blue-black sky,
And banked and dipped and plunged to scavenge flotsam from the swells.

Wild white horses danced themselves to death upon the stony shore,
Headlong, breakneck hurdling, spindrift gambolling, slowed to ambling gait.
A final beach-ward scramble, shallow shingle-churning undertow
That drained their eager gallops into frothy, creamy scallops now
The steeply shelving beach had made their progress more sedate.

Out to sea the night threw muffled echoes at the darkling land.
Wild white horses had been broken, tamed upon the shingle strand.

A COTSWOLD EVENING

Shades of velvet gloaming.
Rolling hills and meadows in the near-departing day.
The honey-coloured cottages reflect the last of light.
Twilight and birdsong; a Cotswold coming night.

Green heights and sheltered valleys.
Villages like Slad, the childhood home of Laurie Lee.
And everywhere the limestone, golden, cream and ochre gilds
The mellow weathered rugged walls of houses, barns and fields.

Ivy-mantled dry-stone:
Unhurried tiny trickling streams meandering along.
Once, underneath a wagon, Rosie's cider sparked a light,
And still Lee's spirit strolls the shades each Cotswold coming night.

HOW VERY ENGLISH

How very lilacs in the spring we are,
How very cricket on the green.
How very salmon and cucumber thins,
How very proud of King and Queen.

How very cream tea Sunday afternoon,
How very croquet on the lawn.
How very jolly hockey sticks – what fun!
How very beige and taupe and fawn.

How very village hall and summer fete,
How very women's institute.
How very roses by a cottage door,
How very twin set and tweed suit.

How very 'hard cheese!' and 'what rotten luck!'
How very 'tally ho, pip-pip!'
How very 'play up, play the game, old chap!'
How very brave stiff upper lip.

How very white cliffs and how boat race day,
How very Henley by the Thames.
How very roast beef and horseradish sauce,
How very country house weekends.

How very Gilbert and how Sullivan,
How very Jeeves and Wooster, too.
How very Noel Coward matinees,
How very tea shoppe rendezvous.

How very 'anyone for tennis, what?'
How very 'stands the clock at three'.
How very Marple and how Mary Meade,
How very 'honey still for tea'.

How very church bells heard across the fields,
How very green and pleasant land.
How very English, and what's wrong with that?
How very English, and how grand!

GLASTONBURY ABBEY

Wild flowers for its altar,
High drifting clouds its roof.
Sad snapped lonely columns –
Abandoned sentinels –
And blankly gaping windows,
A travesty of blinded eyes;
Dissolution's poignant proof.

A once great soaring edifice
Raised up to praise men's deity;
A crumbled broken eloquence
Of crushed and savaged piety.

THE SHORELINE

The shingle tide line stirred its frothing back and forth with every wave,
And bladder wrack, black, shimmer-slimy, stretched its pod fronds in the swell,
While squabbling gulls with black-capped heads flapped, frenzied at the water's edge
In carrion greed as something drowned and bloated gently rose and fell.

Above the tide line stranded wrack and jetsam littered gracelessly,
Abandoned by successive tides, rejected by the sea's disdain.
Dark stinking ooze from outfalls stained the beach head with some nameless waste.
The cleansing sea sweeps twice each day, and each day brings more of the same.

Relentlessly tide's ebb and flow unravels hours from high to low
And back again, and waits for none, and answers only to the moon.
And sometimes calm and sometimes fey, its ways wrapped in such mystery,
While we have still so much to learn, the sea keeps secrets of its own.

SYMBIOSIS

Each noontime I and my packed lunch
Frequent the green where, on a bench
Close by the village pond, I chew
My sandwich and admire the view.

In blissful peace I cogitate,
Philosophise and ponder fate.
Such weighty things I contemplate,
My mind set free to ruminate.

There are some ducks, of which I'm fond,
Which paddle on the lily-pond;
I love their company, indeed,
And bits of sandwich to them feed.

They don't just give their company
For food, though – we're quite close, you see:
We share a wondrous rarity –
A symbiotic empathy!

The spell of this had grown in strength
Until I felt its pull, at length,
So irresistible a bond,
One day I plunged into the pond!

Immersed in their own element,
My head beneath the surface bent
Like theirs, my own world quite forgotten,
I foraged on the murky bottom.

Very soon a fair-sized throng
Had gathered by the lily-pond,
Most, it seemed, to mock and jeer,
Misunderstanding me, I fear.

But we ignored them, one and all,
Those ducks and I, in mutual
Unruffled calm and disregard;
We were as one in kinship shared.

Or so I judged, until I sought
Their innermost and deepest thoughts
And asked them for their views on that;

But all they answered was . . . 'Quack, Quack!'

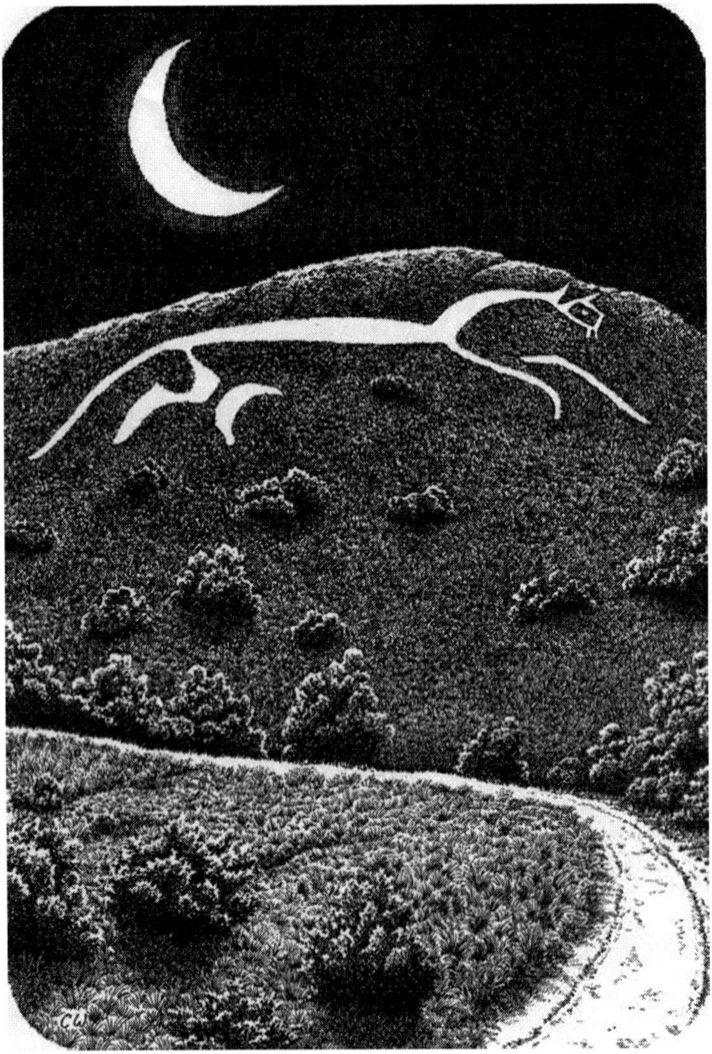

THE WHITE HORSE OF UFFINGTON

King Alfred made me,
Bade me gallop always on these downs.
A sentinel unslumbered
Down centuries unnumbered,
I guard the ancient earthworks
And the sacred burial mounds.

Adzes cut into the turf
And scoured my form
And I was born
From out the gleaming earth.

My spirit is immortal,
Shall guard for evermore –
Long after man no longer cares
To cut the turf and scour.*

* scrape the chalk clean.

(Of all the chalk downs white horses, this one on the Berkshire Downs at Uffington is the best known and most mysterious. Probably not dating *quite* as far back as the time of Alfred The Great, despite local legend, it is generally accepted as the earliest – at least a thousand years old.)

THE WANDERER

One fine morning found a stranger leant against our wall,
As I and John, my brother, went for water from the stream.
He touched a finger to his hat brim. 'Morning, lads,' said he.
'And what a morning, what a day,
and what luck that I came this way.
How else would I have found this handy wall on which to lean?'

Lines like half-formed grins leaked from the corners of his eyes;
A less than sober ploughman might have mapped his furrowed brow.
But, whereas some old faces look like battles long since lost,
The twinkle in his deep-set eyes
Belied a past beset with sighs;
The hardships that he might have known had failed to bring him low.

His smile was like the sky's skin rippling as the sun parts clouds,
Like pie crust over-stretched by all the riches crammed within.
Then, prompted by my brother, John, I asked the stranger's name,
And such a glint of drollery
Was in the gaze he turned on me:
'I have,' he said, 'so many names. Now, where should I begin?

Some call me Jack-o-Lantern, and some others Jack-the-Lad.
To some I'm Jolly Jack Tar, for I've sailed the seven seas.
Jack of all the trades am I, and master of a few.
I'm Jack be nimble, Jack be quick,
Or any name you like to pick.
As long as there's a 'Jack' in it, it's all the same to me.'

He told us that he roamed the land in search of honest toil –
A day's pay for a day's work, and a place to lay his head.
'I asked around the village, and they said to try your farm.
They said your father's hiring.
Would you tell him Jack's enquiring?
But if there's nothing doing, I'll be on my way instead.'

Our mother gave him breakfast, and our father work to do.
It seemed his hands could master any skills that were required.
He mended fences, worked the fields and cut the coppiced beech,
And always with a cheery song
To help the busy day along;
It seemed to us as if life brought him all that he desired.

At supper Jack would join us in the kitchen's homely warmth
And chat before retiring to the hayloft of our barn.
So many tales he had to tell – adventures he had known.
He'd speak of life upon the road,
With lilting voice and eyes that glowed;
Beguiling us for hours, he would spin the finest yarns.

We lads became enchanted by the tales he had to tell
Of strange and daring exploits in all corners of the world,
Of smuggling, poaching, pitting wits against adversity,
And though some tales were far too tall
For words, we half believed them all.
Despite our father's warning winks, we gasped as each unfurled.

But nothing lasts forever and one morning Jack was gone.
He left us with some wistful childish dreams, and little more.
The Jack we knew had many names, and one we hadn't guessed.
For, only after looking back,
We recognised another Jack –
A roguish, restless, feckless, devil-take-thee Jack – Jack Straw.

SOMETHING SENSED AND LOST

Dust-moted August sunlight;
Those grand cream teas on Aunt Maude's clovered lawn.
In mind's eye so much more than harboured memories –
Those pressed leaves saved from golden summer days,
When trees like silhouetted dancers swayed against the glowing sky,
And something more than memories was born.

Those days stay with me, timeless,
Preserved in fading shades of sepia,
When shifting leopard spots of orchard dapple-shade
Played textures of such changing light
On you and me – childlike, but no more childish – quite another us,
So unfamiliar now . . . an enigma.

Down memory's winding distance,
Through long-lost byways only I pursue,
I wander with increasing pensive frequency.
These journeys are warm bonds, not chains,
That tie me to a past of debts that I still owe, but stay unpaid.
Where now, Aunt Maude's cream teas, and where are you?

THE SEA LOCH

The sea loch, burnished silver by the sun,
Smells salt between stern hills on either side,
Whose rugged moss-clad outcrops, green and dun,
Contemplate the slowly turning tide

And trawlers, chugging back and forth, as they
Take trippers out in search of whale and seal.
No longer used for fishing, but for play,
They'd rather have a purpose that was real.

As once they did, before the fishing died,
But now their crewmen sail them just for leisure,
Recalling long-gone days they sailed with pride.
'Of course, it's work,' they shrug, without much pleasure . . .

I wonder if the sea loch and the hills
Regret such changes as the sailors do?
Perhaps they, too, are biding time until
The fish return and trawling starts anew.

THE STREAM OF LIFE

By the bend in the lane at the edge of the wood,
Where the meadow slopes down in an unhurried way
To the moss-shouldered brook with its chuckling flood
Where, in mellow sun shafts, darting damselflies play,

With chanterelle's sweet-smelling spores on the breeze,
And wild honeysuckle draped over a bough,
Here I pause in the dapple-shade cast by the trees
And reflect on the charm of just being here now.

In a tangle of flotsam fetched down by the stream
A swift, furtive scampering catches my eye,
And a bright-eyed plump water vole, wet fur agleam,
Leaps back in the brook with a tail-twitch goodbye.

In the litter of wrack where the vole plunged from sight
Float the spent, sodden husks of a dozen mayfly,
Which broke from the depths for one glorious flight
To mate and then fall where the waiting trout lie.

But nothing in nature is wasted or vain;
What seems to be random unfolds as design.
The purpose in each oddity becomes plain;
From chaos comes order in nature's own time.

A once mighty oak's trunk now bridges the brook,
With its roots reaching skywards, as once did its limbs,
Which carried so safely the nest of the rook
In the strongest of gales, in the wildest of springs.

But now, brought to earth by the storms it once spurned,
Its shattered remains recall greatness long gone;
A home now for fungi and mosses and ferns –
Not death, just the natural way life moves on.

Its saplings now spring from the ground it once ruled,
Their fast-spreading roots laying claim to the earth,
And the glade it left bare, where its shadows once pooled,
Is alive with the lushness of eager rebirth.

So on flows the stream, its renewal assured;
From out of decay, resurrection once more –
Rebirth after each seeming ending endured
In the rich stream of life – nature's endless encore.

NIGHT STORM

The wind was a banshee, a demon of noise
In a sky of a fugitive, cloud-shuttered moon.
A hammer-like downdraft beat onto the moor
With the gauntleted fist of a reiver of doom
That flattened the heather and gorse in its path,
Like a harbinger calling down terrible wrath,
On its way to the crouched valley floor.

The old rusting gate hinges screeched their distress
As the pummelling gusts raked the dark, winding lane,
Snatching the smoke from the hearth as they passed,
And rattling the shuddering door in its frame,
While the hairs on the cat stood on end from its fright,
And the guttering candles blew out, light by light
From the draughts whipping in from the blast.

Then fusillade rods lashed the cottage like shells,
Machine-gunning, strafing, ear-splitting, insane.
The brute wind tossed black clouds all over the sky,
And the ground, overwhelmed by such onslaughts of rain,
Saw the lane become torrent, a wild rushing race,
And the path to the door disappear without trace,
As the gale raged, demented, on high.

The monster thrashed on for the rest of that night
Till, exhausted, it staggered away in the dawn,
And the sky, having wept itself dry, cried no more,
While the land caught its breath, pounded, battered and torn.
And, somehow, the cottage still stood, stone on stone,
Though the roof moss was stripped like flesh pared from a bone –
Stark reminder of nature's raw power.

WHEN SUMMER NEVER CAME

When springtime hid its face,
And winter's unrelenting chill embrace
Still gripped through March and April too,
Till May halfway beguiled us; then summer never came.

Then summer never came,
And sad un-flaming June's raindrop refrain
Dragged soddenly into July,
And more moist airs regaled us, while summer never came.

Still summer never came,
And August drenched our days with endless rain,
And half-sweet, half-forgotten May
Stirred memories to taunt us; still summer never came.

That summer never came.
And then September – here too soon, too wet (again!)
Then talk of Indian summer raised
Some hope of respite from damp days, but on it rained and rained.

October raised anew
Some hope that we might see some skies of blue.
Incredibly, two days passed by
With sunshine from a cloudless sky,
And folks dragged out their rusted barbecues.

And then – that's right – rained out!
Of global warming, desert heat and drought
We heard no more, just talk of rain.
I'll not spend summer here again;
I'm off to find the sun – there is no doubt!

THE POOH-STICK REGATTA

From the rickety bridge by the old watermill
We dropped twigs in the tug of the race,
And shouted encouragement, each to his own,
As our pooh-sticks engaged in the chase.

They battled the treacherous eddies and whorls
On their perilous way to the weir,
As we followed their course in our breathless pursuit
Down the footpath, with cheer after cheer.

By the time they cascaded to white-water doom
No one knew which was which any more,
But each of us swore that his stick had been first,
And declaimed victory with a roar.

THE ENDLESS FLOW

The river sleeks by jettied yachts
Of gin-palatial magnitude,
Past unpretentious houseboat, skiff and barge.
Quite unimpressed by commodores,
All crisply sailor-suity-crewed,
It flows on by with equal disregard.

Ignoring all such fripperies
And self-indulgent vanities,
The river hurries on to meet the sea.
Past locks in tiers and roaring weirs,
And flood defence inanities,
It knows no force can change its destiny.

As old as time, the river's rush
Has seen man's exploits come and go.
Past ford and bridge and dam it courses on.
Past sleepy village, bustling town
The river pours in endless flow,
And surely will long after we have gone.

TINTAGEL

Fourteen centuries gone by.
Now weeds grow high, wild flowers bloom
Where gathered rushes once were strewn
Across the floor of Arthur's hall.

Sheep now graze within the walls,
The ravaged, ivied crumbling shell
Where royal banquets once were held,
With chivalry of old, as legends tell
And, once upon a time, the knights of Arthur dwelled.

Tintagel in Cornwall is claimed by some to be the legendary birthplace of King Arthur.

NOT WISELY, BUT TOO WELL

A bramble-tangle hotchpotch hedge
Of hip and haw and 'old man's beard',
And fruitful elderberry, vetch,
Convolvulus, with trumpets flared
In palely symphonetic stance –
A ragged corps de ballet troupe,
All swaying in a breeze-stirred dance,
While over-ripe blackberries droop
To stain our eager clutching hands,
Which dart, oblivious to thorns,
To pluck from lethal barbed wire strands
Our bloody prizes, shirt sleeves torn.

Next stop, some laden hazel trees,
Whose clustered feather-fronded fruit
Spurs appetites, voraciously
Aroused by nature's boundless loot.
Jaws munching, pockets crammed, we see,
A little further down the lane,
Crab apples in a stunted tree.
Though gorged, we pick them just the same.
Too tempting to resist, despite
The maggots wriggling in each core,
The bitterness of every bite,
We crunch them till our mouths grow sour.

And then, stuffed full, we have to break
And head for home, with belly-ache.

THE DAYS OF INNOCENCE AND DREAMS

Pour me a glass of an oldenday summer;
Lift these tired hours from their midwinter gloom.
Fill me another, sweet-seasoned with spices,
Laced with the freshness of youth's sparkling bloom.

Take back the chill of the creeping of drab years,
Clear past horizons of distant lost dreams.
I, too, was once young and still, in my mind's eye,
Race dragonflies by the bright singing streams.

I turn new-mown hay in the meadows of memory
And lie in the shade of the sweet-smelling sheaves,
Warmed by the sunshine of summer unending –
Summer unending, till innocence leaves.

Once she and I strolled the orchards of springtime,
Breathed in the lilac perfume of the lanes.
That seems so long ago; where did they go to –
Days that we shared, and would not share again?

Where now those lost days of unsullied vision?
Where now the days of those un-shadowed scenes?
Pour one more glass of that oldenday summer,
And let me again dream those innocent dreams.

SUNDAY THINGS

A smoke-blue shimmer hazed the distant slopes.
As Sunday slumbered in the heat,
A church bell's muted, drowsy beat
Told all in gentle murmurings
Of never-changing Sunday things –
Of perpetuity, of dreams and hopes.

Some butterflies explored the meadow blooms,
While iridescent dragonflies
In darting flight bemused our eyes
With jewelled flashings, to and fro,
In sunlight with that certain glow
One only finds on Sunday afternoons.

The scent of buddleia hung on the air –
Delicious breeze-borne headiness
That charmed with mellow muskiness –
While children fashioned daisy rings,
And dreamers dreamed what life might bring,
As Sunday drifted by without a care.

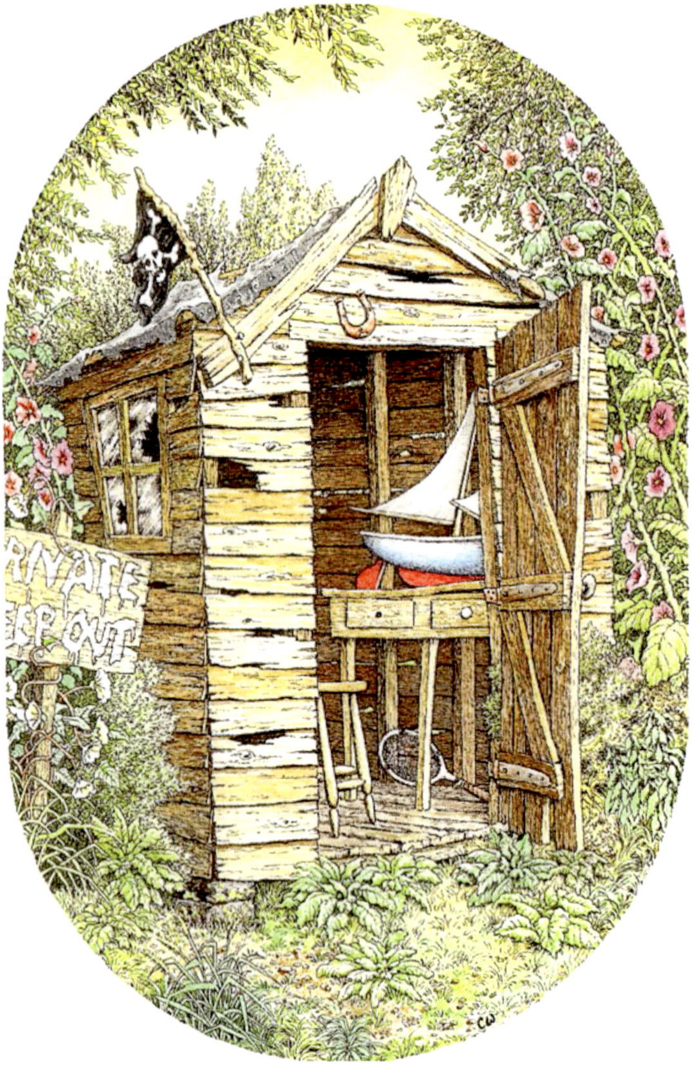

THE OLD BARN

Our 'barn' by the lane leading up to Cobb View,
Was a ramshackle, tired tilting place
In a wilderness patch claimed by nature long since –
Of man's hand now barely a trace –

Surrounded by nettles, chickweed and couch grass,
And dock leaves and brambles and such,
And clambering ivy and 'old man's white beard',
And rife bindweed's smothering clutch.

Wild hollyhocks fought for survival, it seemed,
And leaned on the walls for support,
Or maybe the hollyhocks held up the walls,
Or some mutual respite was sought.

And the cracked painted planks were peeled, blistered and warped,
And the bared and bleached wood showed its years,
And the stacked stones supporting its rickety frame
Were covered with lichen's green tears.

But, though the worn woodwork was rotten with age,
And convolvulus crept through the eaves,
I remember that mouldering pile was a place
Of wonderful, sheer make-believe.

That 'barn' could be castle or dungeon or yacht,
Or a pirate ship sailing the main,
Or a western saloon, a spaceship to the moon,
Or a goldmine or runaway train.

We foraged the countryside, lived off the land –
Whatever the seasons would yield –
Then met in our 'barn' to share what had been found
In hedgerow and orchard and field.

We called it our barn – that old tumbledown shed –
A grandiose name for a shack.
It was magical then, and I still feel its spell,
Even now, every time I think back.

DAWN MIST

The hills roll gently,
Swelling from horizon to horizon,
Each tree-crowned crest
An enigmatic silhouette
Emerging from the lazy mist
That lingers in each sleepy cleft.

The mist wraiths melt in tendrils
Drawn to sky by rising heat,
And, effortlessly, great red kites
Ride the thermals up to heights
Not even soaring larks can beat.

Dawn mist gives way
To full-blown day.

THE GALLEON MOON

In the wine-like glow of evening light
The swifts and martins sweep the sky,
Then a galleon moon sails seas of night,
While fire-ship stars in her wake drift by,

With cloaking darkness held at bay
By dreams of innocence till day –
Those dreams that fade in dawn's half light,
Whose spells can only charm by night –
When the galleon moon, her voyage done,
Makes landfall on the beach of dawn.

In the wine-like glow of infant day
The lark soars skies of crystal light,
And the fire-ship stars have sailed away
With the galleon moon to another night.

INNOCENCE RECALLED

An autumn of rich memories is mine.
Like wind-blown leaves that drift on by
And, rustling, age but never die,
I hold them to the light, and still they shine.

A well remembered landscape comes to mind:
A summer day, some breeze-borne seeds,
A shaded stream bank fringed with reeds,
And something childhood's wonder left behind.

I see us once again in clear recall
As fingers brushed against a palm
Unwitting, we two arm in arm,
Quite unaware of what might yet befall.

That childlike innocence could ever leave
Was nonsense on that summer day,
The loss of dreams still far away
And, looking back, it's hard, still, to believe.

Where ignorance was bliss, still folly came
And stole away the innocence,
And reason took the place of sense,
And nothing then could ever be the same.

My autumn of such memories sustains,
Undimmed by all the passing years,
Unclouded now by former fears,
And what was lost to us, to me remains.

THE KINGFISHER

Where light meets the swift stream
And shatters to crystal,
To dance like ice sparks on the chattering flow,
The sapphire kingfisher
Streaks into the torrent
With unerring aim at the dartings below.

The blue iridescence,
A flash by the river,
Spells death to its prey from the dagger-like bill.
With each lightning plummet
The sapphire assassin,
This king of all fishers, claims yet one more kill.

DANCING IN THE DARK

Star-moths nibbled at the night's dark curtain,
Puncturing the fabric, letting in a million sparks
That coruscated like a stage of dancers,
Whose practised choreography enchanted by their dancing in the dark.

Fireflies mirrored in a pool at midnight
Seemed to imitate the stars parading in their arc,
Like tiny lamps reflected in the water
In miniature performances, impersonating dancers in the dark.

Then, as darkness paled away to sunrise,
One by one they winked out to the last extinguished spark,
And stars and fireflies left their stage till nightfall
When, once again they'd face the footlights, imitating dancers in the dark.

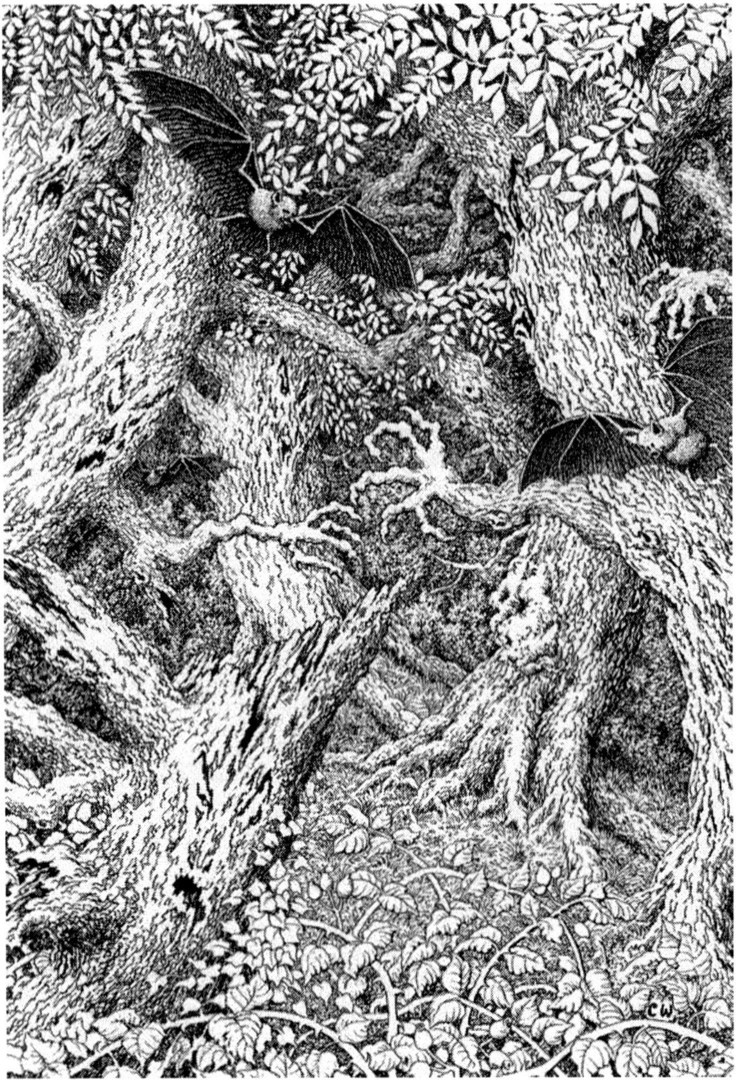

THE DREAD BEAST OF NIGHT (a Gothic homage!)

On the rim of the world sank a blood-red sun,
Whose skyfire devoured a pale, blinded moon.
In a valley crouched under a molten-edged hill,
Dark-dappled with shadows, and darkening still,
I had lingered till twilight, immersed in the spell
Of the day's dwindling hours in this beautiful vale.
But, as darkness deepened, I felt an unease,
And some nameless fear came to me on the breeze.
Then, where had been peace and content solitude,
An eerie disquiet replaced my calm mood.
The last air of birdsong had suddenly ceased,
And an unearthly silence soft-sighed its release.
It lasted long moments in unnerving pause,
As the dread beast of night stirred, unsheathing dark claws.
Then the shattering clatter of bats taking flight,
Like panicking shadows unleashed by the night,
Burst into the stillness and beat at the sky,
As in demon delight that the sun had to die.
To my ears came a slyness of dark whisperings;
A skin-crawling rasping, like unfolding wings.
Was that mere insect scutter so close to my head,
Or could it be something more dreadful instead?
Then I shrank from the chill of some evil embrace
Whose vile tendrils reached out and brushed at my face,
And I turned like a coward to flee in my fright,
And left that dark place to the dread beast of night.

DAWN AND FADING STARS

Ghosts of constellations prick the young dawn's outmost height –
Melting ice-white crystals from night's crown,
Stars of distant galaxies whose roles are played by night,
Their curtain fall has once more come around.

The waking sky's a backdrop stained gradated shades of blue,
Sun-washed, too bright for constellations now,
But hidden, patient in the wings, they simply wait their cue
For curtain-rise and one more star-filled show.

Though, westerly by moon-speed, other eyes can see them glow;
Undimmed, they hang in sparkling chandeliers,
And in an earthspin's few short hours the day will take its bow
And exit as the starlight reappears.

FRINTON

Frinton slumbers in its past,
Retreating picturesquely from today.
Shunning piers and fish and chips,
A brash fairground and boating trips,
And hotel terraces that cause dismay,
Let Frinton keep its charms just as they are.

Developers will kindly keep away.

NIGHT GLADES

Decked in silvered flecks of moonlight
Stippling through the shifting shadecast,
Woodland glades lie stilled and dreamlike,
Hushed and waiting while the dew breath
Tinsels every leaf and fern frond
As slow moments steal to midnight.

Nightjar's churring song and owl-call
Serenade a gibbous moon now;
Light-shy creatures stirred by nightfall
Fill the glades with furtive rustlings.
Slyly swift between the moon darts,
Hunter, prey match skills as rivals.

Through the tree crowns moonlight lances
Cast their ever-changing patterns,
Splashing shafts in jewelled dances,
While the moisture-laden night air
Softly sets in beads of dew gems,
As the stealth of dawn advances.

So the moon pales, drained of splendour;
Night glades wake from fitful slumber.

PICA PICA (The Magpie)

There is no doubt the magpie's shout
Suits him so well, the oafish lout;
He struts the rooftops, fields and woods,
While using language no bird should.

It's true I love the magpie not;
He squawks and talks such tommyrot,
Upsets the other birds a lot –
Gets doves under their collars hot.

No rhyme or reason to his mood,
He's just bad-tempered, mean and rude.
A course of anger management
For magpies would be heaven-sent.

Unsettling to the nerves is he,
Dive-bombing from a wayside tree.
His sudden 'Chacka-chacka chack!'
Sounds like a maxim gun attack.

A thief as well, this screeching pest,
Who steals the eggs from others' nests.
All in all, I must admit,
I like him not a little bit.

TWO GREEDY OWLS

Two owls met for lunch – or it may have been brunch –
In a tree at the edge of a forest.
Alfresco they dined, being both so inclined,
One named Magnus, the other named Horace.

After field mice and vole, which they gobbled up whole,
They polished off several escargots,
Then a brace each of weasels they spied in some teasels,
For their taste buds perceived no embargoes.

The time ticked to two as their appetites grew,
Right along with the girth of their tummies,
Then a couple of pheasant were found very pleasant;
'I say!' they both cried, 'Simply yummy!'

By now it was four, and still they craved more –
Those two greedy owls, H and M.
A party of hares was caught quite unawares,
And soon there was no trace of them.

Around about seven it seemed gourmet heaven,
As an unwary fox was dispatched,
Then some beaver and stoat and a wandering goat,
So ill-fated to stray on their patch.

Then the silver moon rose, and you might just suppose
That these two were replete from their snacking,
But a large flock of geese made a succulent feast;
'Jolly good!' they both screeched, 'Oh, how cracking!'

Just escaped from a zoo, a runaway gnu
Passed their way, to his cost – how distressing.
It took nigh an hour for the owls to devour,
But the flavour was quite prepossessing.

It was midnight by now, and a ruminant cow
Chewed its last cud, I'm sorry to say.
Now feeling quite bloated, the greedy pair voted
'Twas high time to call it a day.

On the distant horizon a small herd of bison
Appeared on the wide moonlit plain.
Said Magnus with sorrow, 'I'm stuffed till tomorrow!'
'Me too,' Horace said, 'What a shame!'

'I'm full to the gill, but it's been such a thrill.
Dining out's a delightful pursuit.'
'Let's do it again,' proposed M to his friend.
'Oh, how topping,' cried H, 'What a hoot!'

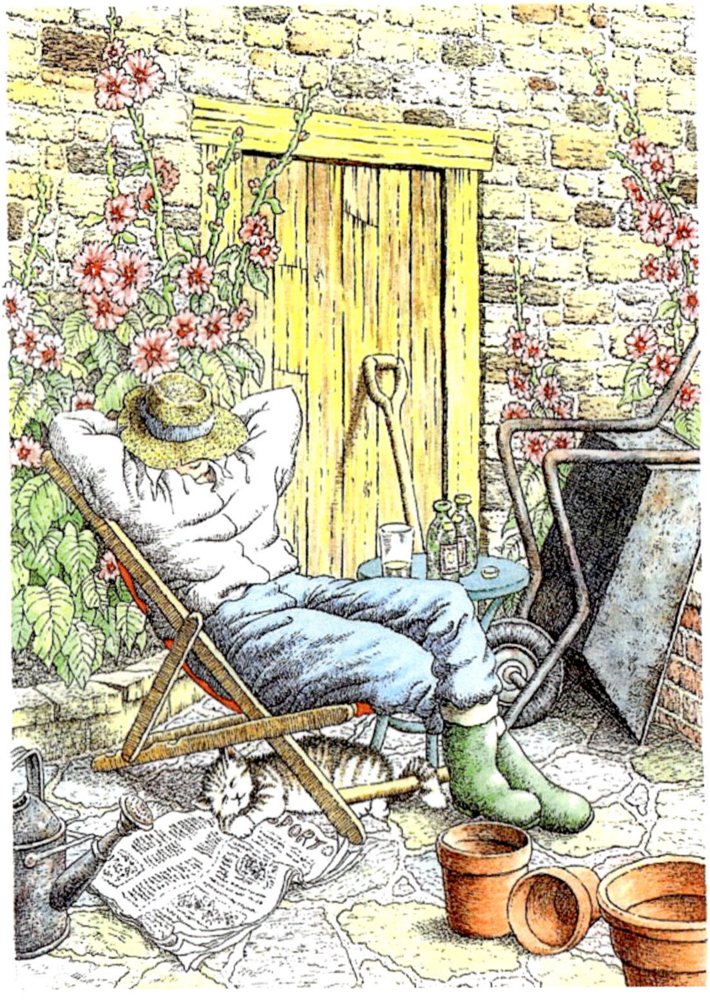
SPORT

GARDENING BREAK

The wheelbarrow leans on the old garden wall;
It's been there since daybreak, not moving at all.
The village church clock chimes the hours away,
And an old man sits watching some dandelions sway.
When Granddad came round at the first crack of dawn
He said he'd do weeding and then mow the lawn.
He went to the shed, got out barrow and mower,
Then ate Mum's fried breakfast, which took him an hour.
He fetched out a deckchair and dozed for a while;
'To aid the digestion,' he said, with a smile.
Around about eight he stood up, stretched and yawned,
Then leaned on the barrow and gazed at the lawn.
He took off his hat, scratched his head thoughtfully,
Then called out to Mum, 'Any chance of some tea?'
His thirst quenched, he sat for a little while longer,
Scratching his chin, clearly having a ponder.
Then, eyes lighting up, to the shed he withdrew,
And found some beer left from the last barbecue;
Took the newspaper, reading the sports page at length,
Then had forty winks to recover his strength.
Tired out from watching all Granddad's exertions,
The cat wandered out of a patch of nasturtiums.
On the crumpled newspaper a soft bed he made
And proceeded to snooze in the deckchair's cool shade.
'Off to the shop,' Mum called, 'Need one or two things.
Just be a minute. Now, don't overdo things!'
When Mum came back she found Granddad awake,
Having strolled up the garden to lean on the gate.
'How's it all going?' she asked, with a hunch
There'd not be much action till after his lunch.
After some sandwiches, tea and a bun
Granddad relaxed in the afternoon sun,
Planning the best way to tackle the lawn.

Till drowsiness filled him and, with a great yawn,
He crossed one leg over the other and sighed,
'I'll just have five minutes.' 'Oh sure,' Mum replied.

The shadows have lengthened, the lawn still unmown;
Perceptibly higher have dandelions grown.
'It's teatime!' calls Mum, waking Granddad, still yawning.
'Let's call it a day. Finish off in the morning!'

PART TWO

THE SEASONS

SPRING, AT LAST

The sky is drawn-together brows,
A darkened corrugated frown,
Drear and sagging, leached of light
And promising just sepia monotony.

If only Dufy's brush could browse
These dragging days of monochrome;
But colour's still a cuckoo-flight
From saturated, introverted February.

Winter's palette seems eternal,
Mixed only with tones of grey
And shades of waiting, hues of doubt –
Nocturne after nocturne, seeming almost seamless.

Just when gloom appears perpetual,
All of colour washed away,
Snowdrops, crocuses peep out;
New sap begins to course and, once again, greenness!

OF THINGS TO COME

The timid warmth of early spring
Had gently teased frostgrip from shuttered earth,
And now the scents of wakened loam
And autumn's leaf mould stirred like broken dreams.

New buds shrugged through their overcoats
And rumoured nature's miracle rebirth,
As winter's gaunt and starky trees
Now clothed their nakedness with gauzy greens.

From sleep, lit by the spark of spring,
Their branches glowed with flames of pale green fire,
And infant hours of sunlight grew
To days of glimmerings of things to come.

From fossilled and suspended time,
As each day stoked the heat of winter's pyre,
The landscape yawned and stretched and smiled,
And every bud and shoot reached for the sun.

SPRING BLOOMS

The frost-sequinned copse stirs to blue-shadowed dawn,
Whose pale timid spring sun grows stronger each day.
Beneath the bare branches the strengthening light
Wakes celandine, snowdrops from winter's long night,
And drab months of darkness no longer hold sway.

And soon wood anemone's white buds appear –
The windflower's delicate star carpet glows.
The ancient glades fill with its musky perfume
That hangs on the air until columbines bloom
Beside purple orchid and yellow primrose.

Then May's bluebell drifts lace the air with their scent,
And the woodland floor shimmers with dappled blue light.
The heady bouquet clouds perception until
The mind swims unchecked as its senses unreel.
Then the rife dandelions spread their golden delight.

As the tender young leaves of the beeches unfurl,
And shade slowly spreads where the sunlight has been,
The canopy soon overshadows each glade,
And then woodland's spring blooms must wither and fade,
As their colours give way to the summer's deep green.

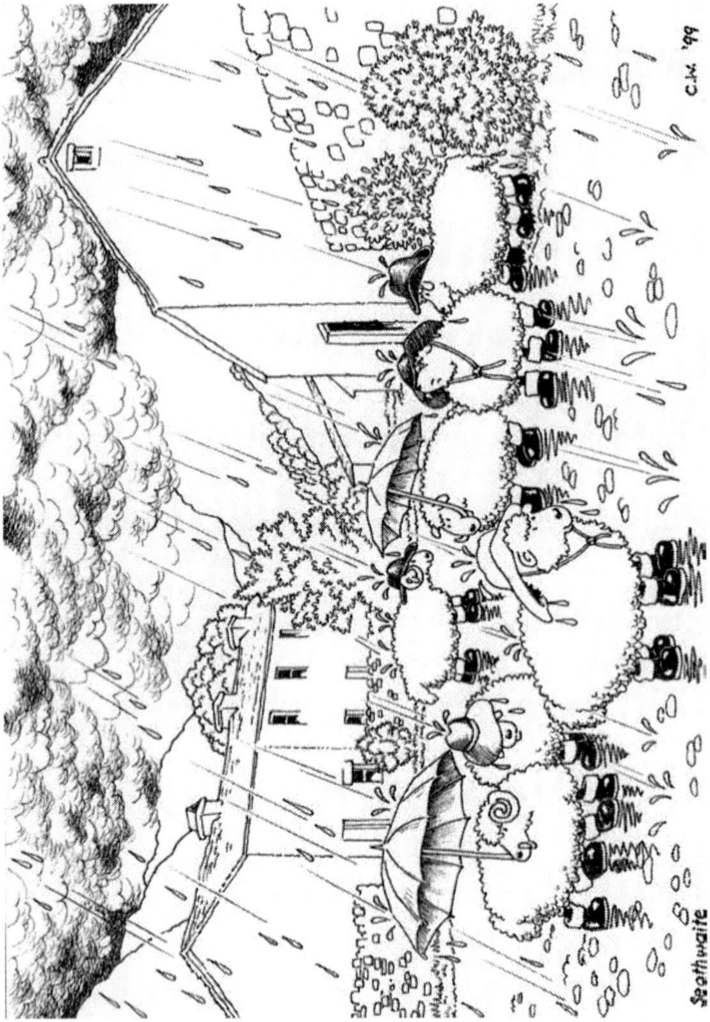
Seathwaite

SPRINGTIME IN SEATHWAITE

Oh, Seathwaite, your fame's envied not
By any other Lakeland spot
For, whereas others have their share
Of rain, mixed in with weather fair,
No place in Cumbria I know
Compares with you for H_2O!

As winter turns to soggy spring
The rain stops and monsoons begin.
The clouds deposit endlessly
What's sucked up from the Irish Sea,
And then the downpours turn quite frantic –
More comes from the North Atlantic!

The 'sea' in Seathwaite is so apt,
Since in its formula you're wrapped;
Your highest ever inches' score
Was two-five-seven in 'fifty four,
Though most years you claim, modestly,
One-seventy (metres – four point three).

That's fourteen feet, plus inches two,
Or, head to tail, three herdwick ewe –
Quite enough to put a damper
On the most intrepid camper.
What a record, Seathwaite, moist –
So, elsewhere is m*y* camping choice.

REBIRTH

The constant weathering of wind and rain,
The alternating till of freeze and thaw,
The labours of the humble, tireless worm
Make friable the stirring earth once more.

In autumn ploughshares carved and turned its flesh
And bared its bones to raucous gull and crow;
Now, after winter's brittle crystal grasp,
Mothballed machines return to drill and sow.

Aroused from hibernation, engines roar:
Leviathans revive the drowsing land,
While daylight's waxing hours warm up the soil
And break the grip of February's hand.

The rain – no longer winter-barbed – brings cheer
To orchards pruned in January chill,
Whose new-grown shoots soon bud and bear the bloom
Of infant fruit that summer days will swell.

Forgotten now, drab winter's dreary days,
As meadows stretch and revel in the sun,
And springing from the newly woken earth
Come vigour, life and colour where was none.

Rekindled patchwork quilts of ancient fields
Absorb the surging lifeblood of rebirth,
While rippling, lacy skeins of homing birds
Cast flitting shadow-play across the earth.

The suns of southern lands have warmed their wings;
Now, northwards, irresistibly, they're drawn
In ragged arrowheads of flagging flight,
That magnetism once again reborn.

Now winter-dormant creatures reappear,
As thicket, hedge and coppice burst to green.
The pulse of new life quickens day by day
In field and woodland, river, lake and stream.

The land takes on a spruce and vibrant glow,
And all the weald's refreshed and shimmering.
The miracle of rebirth casts its spell,
As springtime weaves its wonder once again.

DOWNLAND HEDGEROWS

The lane winds its unhurried way between the fields of spring-green wheat,
Bounded by tall hedgerows twined with brambles, lilac and wild rose,
And elderberry's rosette blooms of perfect froths of creamy lacings –
Breeze-stirred heads of florets curtseying in graceful nodding shows.

Below the beech-crowned ridge the down slopes steeply to the hedge-lined fields.
A living archaeology of leaf and wildlife still survives
In every hedgerow in this patchwork landscape, old as time itself-
Safe havens still for moth and robin, shrews, voles, hedgehogs, butterflies.

All around the fields of wheat, new crops now chequer downland scenes –
Citric rash of rapeseed yellow, blue of linseed, spreading fast –
Displacing year on year now more and more of what we used to see.
At least let's save the hedgerows, so their priceless heritage will last.

SKIDDAW CLOUDS, APRIL

Grey, belly-sagging clouds swoop down,
Impale themselves on Skiddaw's crown
And, like some over-zealous tide,
Spread jealous tendrils down his side,
As if, in envy, to deny
His very presence in their sky.

As smoking wraiths enshroud his height
And hide the Derwent fells from sight,
The Lakeland weather closes in,
To cloak all in oblivion
And, like some bleak, unyielding wall,
Denies the climb to one and all.

LATE SPRING, EVENING

On a spell-cast, lilac-scented late spring breeze,
Drifts the drowsy, lulling hum of tireless bees,
And a tractor's distant, muffled, thrumming drone,
As old Thomas, day done, heads once more for home.

And now evening's orchestrated serenade
Charms with such familiar sweet notes, softly played:
All around, the crickets' muted buzzing call;
Sleepy fields away, a wistful, dreamy peal –

Tolling bells in somnolence at evensong,
Calling gently to the faithful few to come.
Old Tom will, I know, be sure to hurry there,
Once again to practise with the village choir.

Hoarsely, from across the shadowed orchards now,
Come the rasping cries of homing rook and crow,
As the sunset's palette paints the glowing sky
With a vivid, fiery Turneresque goodbye.

In the village, cottage lights begin to shine,
As shadows swiftly gather in the day's decline.
The dewy evening air is sweetly redolent
With plum and pear and apple blossom's heady scent.

In gathering evening's fast enclosing arms, once more
Ceaselessly the swifts and martins swoop and soar,
And ghostly day-shy supper-seeking bats flit by,
Silent, radar-sure against the darkling sky.

As the ever-deepening blue-grey shadows fall,
Close by I hear a neighbour's quiet, friendly call;
I turn and wave, exchange a warm, polite 'goodnight',
And then stand savouring the swiftly dimming light,

Still relishing the lovely fading scene, until
The evening's rising breeze begins to damp and chill.
And then, with a final, lingering farewell,
I, too, yield at last to night's call, with a smile.

AN ENCHANTMENT

The sleepy glade basked warmly in the sun-washed April afternoon,
And drowsy drone of insects lulled and charmed,
And heady scents of bluebells and wild honeysuckle filled the air,
While in my mind the strangest music formed.

Random seeming wind-sung notes played gently through the sighing leaves,
A rustling, soft impromptu overture
Like no song ever penned, an orchestration by the gentlest breeze,
Composed by nature's hand, artlessly pure.

The silver chuckling of an unseen rill somewhere beyond the trees
Joined in with counterpoint, it seemed to me,
And suddenly I knew I'd never heard such lovely music played;
No human ever had such artistry.

Adrift in timeless interlude, reality suspended now,
All senses hypnotised by nature's spell,
I revelled in the magic of a symphony without compare,
A captive to enchanted hours until,

As daylight dwindled into dusk, and cloaking shadows gathered round,
The breeze fell and the tune began to fade,
But, as I wandered homeward, my mind swam still with the sweetest notes –
The haunting music of that April glade.

SPRING MAGIC

The breeze-stirred shade-cast rained sun-puddles
Down the winding beech-lined lane
In shifting pools of liquid light
That caused the eye bemused delight,
Like impish sprites the senses sought to comprehend in vain.

Above my head the arching branches
Formed a rustling cool arcade –
A coruscating canopy
Of restless whispering greenery
That showered sequin sun-drops like a ticker-tape parade.

Between the beeches, heady-scented
Buddleia and lilac blooms
Drew questing butterfly and bee
To find a nectar treasury
In glorious profusion, with the sweetest of perfumes.

To either side, beyond the beeches,
Orchards spread their blossom shade,
Their subtler fragrance more refined –
Champagne, compared to rich red wine –
The genteel essence of each spring no years could ever fade.

Each season of the year brings pleasures,
But, when spring sun lights the lanes,
And blossom bouquet fills the air,
I know that nothing can compare
With springtime, as its pure enchantment weaves its spell again.

THE MEADOW BANK

The teasing wind breathes puckish ruffs
Through feathered heads of meadow grass,
And drowses round the willow hems with idly stroking fingertips.
The stream laps gently at its banks
And chuckles in its crystal throat,
While lofty nodding reedmace sway beneath the breeze's brushing lips.

Pale fleecy parasols of clouds
Trail lazy shadows in their wake
Across the gently basking fields, to melt like fancies in the stream.
Stone-still as any obelisk,
A patient, stilt-like heron waits
With eyes that scan the shallow flow and seek the darting dace's gleam.

From deep within a dock leaf's shade
Two tiny furtive glints appear
And, whiskers twitching, warily a field vole eyes a circling hawk.
The susurrating breeze's sigh
Is perforated raucously,
As perfect peace is splintered by a squabbling magpie's fishwife squawk.

A startling flash of black and white,
The magpie scolds the world at large;
No seeming reason for its ire – just evil temper, plain and pure.
The soaring kestrel drifts away;
The field vole blinks and breathes once more.
A bright streak flashes in the stream; the heron's strike is swift and sure.

A VILLAGE MORNING, SUMMER

Mist wraiths rise like kindled fires as early sun warms wooded hillsides;
Smoke-haze blue against the sky, pale impish sprites that vaporise,
Mere phantom wisps, dissolved by rising warmth and distance, lost to sight,
Left far behind the lark's steep climb beyond the reach of human eyes.

A cockerel's crow is echoed by another, far across the fields,
While dew-sweet, sun-warmed hedgerow blossoms tempt some early butterflies.
The sleepy village stirs itself and, yawning, picturesquely wakes.
A summer day unfolds its charms beneath the tranquil Kentish skies.

Above the rolling fields the ridge of Warren View looks over Shorne.
The miller climbs his post-mill steps, the breeze set fair to turn the vanes.
Up Tanyard Hill a team of shires is led at steady, plodding pace
Among dust-sequinned sun shafts through the dapple-shade along the lanes.

In jostling chatter-bicker groups the children make their way to school,
While signs are turned to 'OPEN' at the Post Office and grocer's store.
The blacksmith lights the charcoal, and then pumps the bellows at the forge
To fashion white-hot ingots into horse-shoes, sickles, nails galore.

The landlord at the Rose and Crown rolls barrels off the brewer's dray.
The church clock chimes the strokes of nine, then ticks to ten with no great haste.
Old Ambrose sucks an empty pipe and dozes by the water trough.
The village day unfolds itself at peaceful and unhurried pace.

70

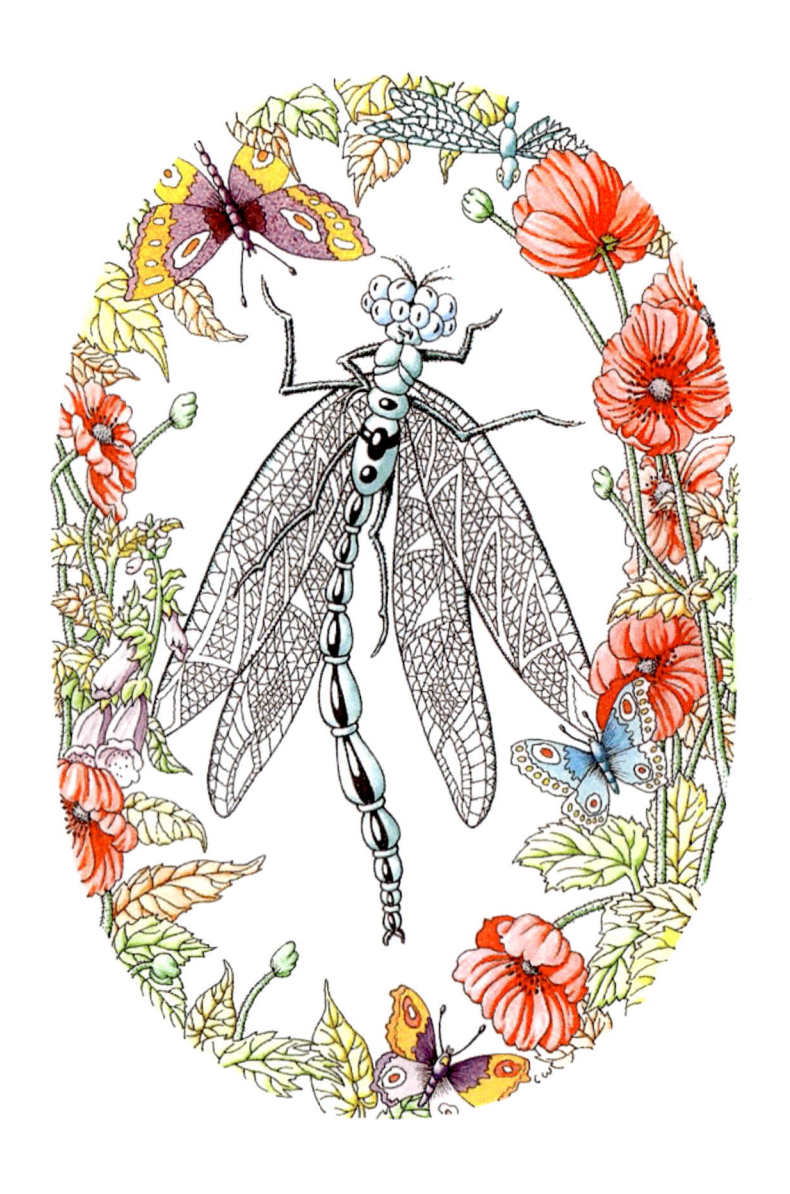

THE DRAGONFLY

Beneath a shady oak I sat
And contemplated this and that
Beside a lily-covered pond,
Where willows trailed their graceful fronds.

A dragonfly swooped down to me
And, brightly iridescent, he –
Or she, I'm not sure which, it's true –
Gazed up at me with eyes of blue.

Then hypnotised, as in a trance,
Did I return its steady glance,
And eye to eye to eye to . . . 'Why
So many, Dragonfly?' asked I.

'Oh, human,' answered he (or she),
'I need so many eyes to see
The menaces that lie beyond
The sanctuary of my pond.

This world, for you, is safe, I know,
But I'm so tiny, and I glow
So brightly that the birds can see
I'm prey, and they hunt down poor me.'

'Dear Dragonfly,' I said to him
(Or her, still quite confused and dim),
'I see now why so many eyes
Are needed for you dragonflies.'

A HOUSE MARTIN SUMMER

Underneath the broad-spread reed thatch eave
Warm shadows drape, mauve-grey against the sun-bleached wall,
And tiny flask-like mud adobes cleave –
Fortress villages of nests, immune to gravity and all.

From Africa they came to England's spring,
Drawn irresistibly by nature's urgent claim.
Cliff dwellers once, now these eave nesters cling
Beneath this reed thatch – seemingly, to them it's all the same.

From a coppice spiral haze-blue skeins;
A charcoal stack is firing black inside its turf-clad mound,
And, in between the patchwork fields, the lanes
Wind tranquilly to manor, church, the village green and pond.

Over all the martins swoop and soar –
Through the haze-veiled coppice, over farmland, stream and lane,
Till summer's dwindling days see them no more.
The broods all fledged, now warmer lands have drawn them south again.

THE LOCK

A country lock, midsummer;
Weather perfect for a river day.
But what a vast armada on the stream –
The drop to surface from the quay,
Reducing with the flooding ride,
Packed with a flotilla
Rising slowly on the man-made tide.

Queues of cruisers,
Narrow-boats,
Lined up above,
Lined up below,
All waiting for the gates
To open, let the flow
Take each one where they wished to go.

And just how many in that throng
Had noticed damsel fly or water vole
The while they rushed along?

INTERLUDE

Where the breeze-stirred willows trail lace fingers in the lazy flow,
And burnished damselflies dart like quicksilver,
Where lush swaying meadow grass and flaunting poppies wave and bow
By chuckling waters rich with trout and elver,
Here lies sheer delight in idling out a shameless tranquil hour –
A self-indulgent luxury of time.
And, what if that hour should stretch to two or three, or even more?
I feel no guilt – these dawdling hours are mine.

The river bank is edged with purple loosestrife's soft magenta haze,
And parasols of giant cow parsley soar,
While parachutes of dandelion drift by in vagabond displays,
And cuckoo pint un-sheaths its brazen lure.
My back against a chestnut's bole, my shade its rustling canopy,
The scent of creamy-yellow meadowsweet
Wafts, delicate as childhood's half remembered, half dreamed imagery,
Where crowding strands of recollections pleat.

From riffling grass, with piping call, a rising meadow pipit sings,
Then swoops to earth with lower, liquid tune.
With rippling song and higher flight, a distant speck on tireless wings,
A skylark cues the fast approaching noon.
Spinning out this interlude of unrepentant indolence,
As lazy afternoon drifts by about me,
I feel for those weighed down by days unlit by all this recompense –
Such days may make their dismal way without me.

Too soon late afternoon unwinds to mellow twilight shadow-play,
The air beguiled by honeysuckle musk.
A dwindling frill of light left from the hem of near-departed day
Leads homeward through the ever deepening dusk.

THE SENTINEL

Beside a pleasant shaded stream that dawdled drowsily,
I strolled the afternoon away in mellow golden light.
The day and I had wandered with no sense of urgency,
Ahead of us the prospect of a warm and tranquil night.

But suddenly a movement by the stream's edge caught my eye.
The dipping sun's rays sparked off something glitteringly bright,
A dazzling stop-start zigzag flash of burnished energy –
A dragonfly, that harlequin of darting sequinned flight.

In frenzied bursts of dizzy speed, the brilliant creature dashed,
Quartering the idling brook as if a thing possessed.
I marvelled at its energy, such aerial panache,
Its single-minded purpose, that it never paused for rest.

That pleasant stretch of stream side was the dragonfly's domain,
The place he'd picked to guard against all others of his kind.
Until a likely mate should chance his way for him to claim,
The dragonfly would know no rest or any ease of mind.

I watched him for an hour and then turned and went my way,
Leaving him on guard there in the slowly fading light,
That sentinel patrolling with such scintillant display –
That dragonfly, that harlequin of darting sequinned flight.

SUNLIGHT ON A SYCAMORE

Honey bees wove gauzy sound,
A soothing one-key composition,
Lulling, tranquillising music,
Mesmerising, soporific –
Plainchant in a meadow found.

Shifting dapple-splash displays
Of leopard spots and tiger stripes
Played beneath a sycamore,
Whose rustling leaves sighed soft encores
And laced the shade with mote-filled rays.

Split by darting shafts of light,
The shadows twined a dance of veils,
Snapping sunbeams into tracer –
Sequin-glitter rain like lasers –
Tinselled dizzying delight.

Sunlight through the sycamore
Made dazzling spangles dance like sprites,
Bemusing choreography,
Kaleidoscopic fantasy –
A ceaseless incandescent shower.

CHILDHOOD'S LAST SUMMER

Summer blood sang in each one of us.
Dull school's prison gates flung wide,
Now on freedom's swelling tide
We rode the rushing crests with childhood's lust.

Term's last bell had sounded liberty.
Out of mind now chalk and cane
And sun-dreams baked on window panes;
Emancipation gulfed exultantly.

Skinny hens scratched in the dusty lane
And scattered as we ran for bliss,
And chased the girls to steal a kiss,
Towards the sun-soaked weeks, joy unrestrained.

Scuttling through the village to our teas
Of marge and jam on crusty bread,
While plans of action filled each head –
We boys would meet at six at Green Farm Leas.

The carefree hedonistic days flew by –
No lane or byway left un-trod,
No meadow, river bank or wood –
We raised up freedom's grail and drank it dry.

And so that last blithe summer drifted on.
The last? In mind's eye, bitter-sweet,
Because the next June I would meet
The glorious Lavinia Lauriejohn!

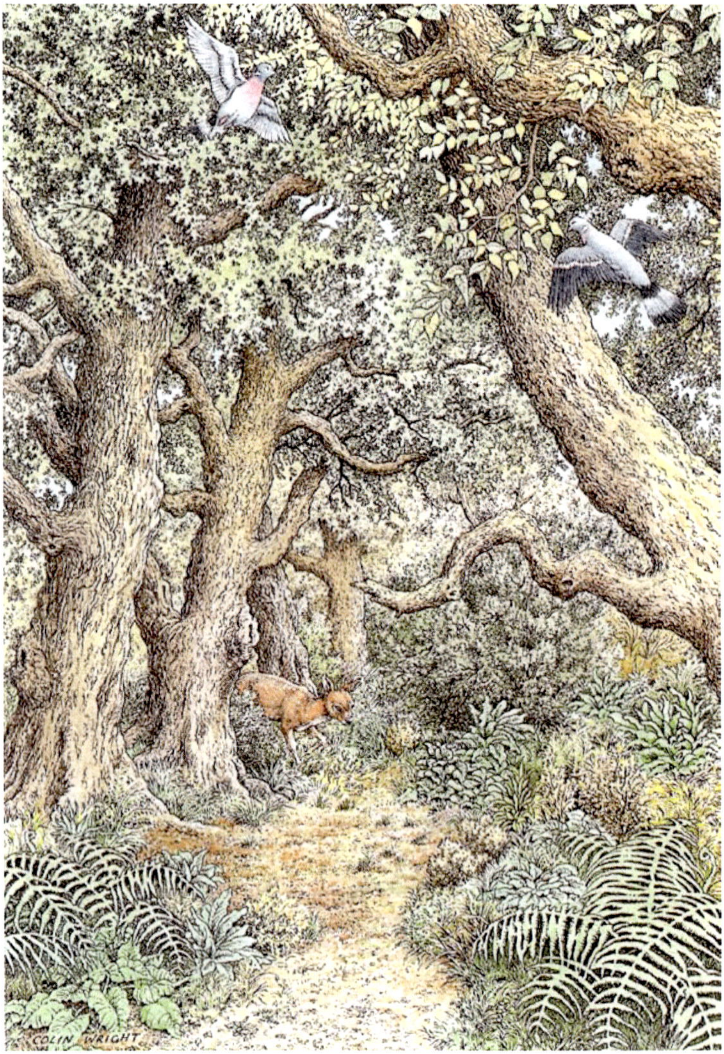
COLIN WRIGHT

A FOREST SPELL

At the forest's shaded rim
In mottling, dancing sunlight lancings,
Standing paused, my breath drawn in,
A pulse-held listening, soft-sighed rustlings,
Treetop bustlings, warm breeze hustling.
Here in flickering half-light hovering
Seems enchantment, peace, contentment,
Spellbound glory, sanctuary.
Bewitched, I'm held in empathy
With all I find surrounding me.
Then a furtive small commotion
Breaks this tranquil meditation:
In a blur of graceful motion,
Timid, darting animation,
Steals a faun, all sharp-eyed caution,
In an instant lost to vision.
Onward then, the magic beckoning,
Dappled winding ways meandering
In between the mighty towering
Oaks and beeches, sun-spears showering.
I am lost in musing wandering,
Senses widening, senses reeling,
Senses marvelling, captive, wondering.
Soaring trunks with creepers clinging,
Ferns unfurling, upward straining,
Seeking sun-darts, brightly glancing,
Filled with dust motes' dizzy dancing.

Soon a glade's edge beckons brightly;
Here I pause to linger quietly
In a sun-washed brackened dell,
Lost to time in nature's spell.

SUMMER ENCOUNTERS

Shaded in this forest greenglow church-calm sanctuary stillness,
Couched on yielding moss which smells of summerness and slow decay,
Eyes half-closed, I drifting-listen to the stirrings, rustlings, bustling
Life within the damp leaf litter, busy insect skitterpatter,
Sheltered from the sunscorched day.

Distantly, a lesser-spotted, prospecting some bark for termites,
Punctuates my random musings, punching holes in daydream peace,
Staccato-stitching hems of moments, threads that link segments of silence,
Muted, far-off stammering – insistent, though, in hammering
Home his point in sundry trees.

A dragonfly darts through a sunshaft, comes, for no apparent reason,
To an iridescent full stop, sequin-patterned by the sun;
Captured in the mote-swirled spotlight like a turquoise-spangled actor
Skilled in arts of stage deception, playing still-life to perfection
To an audience of one.

Here, with infant ferns unfolding, spreading gauzy fronds like lacework,
Reaching for the sun's cascading glint and gleam of splashing light,
Face to face, a hover-wasp and I commune in stand-off study,
Search for meaning in each other, until – losing interest –
He abandons me for flight.

THE INLAND SEA

The wind-stirred sun-sheened surface of the meadow undulates –
A rippling, whispering, dry-waved inland sea –
From river bank to woodland edge, with pitching toss and trough,
In restless, rhythmic, rolling symmetry.

No sharp and salty tang or sparkling splash of ocean spray
Hangs on the air about this land-locked sea,
And breeze-blown froth of parasols of seeds and gossamer
Replaces spindrift's creamy filigree.

No flashing dip and soar of gulls, but darting dragonflies,
Like iridescent impish pimpernels;
No crash of rushing combers on a silvered, windswept strand,
But softly ruffled, rustling grassy swell

Breaking at the meadow's shore on dunes of tansy gold,
And green-clad reefs and crags of woodland trees,
While poppies ride the rolling crests of meadowsweet and rye
In dancing scarlet flotsam revelries.

Washed by these dry whispering waves, with goldenrod for kelp,
No jetsam of sea glass and shining shells,
No bladder wrack or cliff-clung gorse, or sea anemone;
Instead, field wood-rush, hawkweed and harebells.

Now, drifted by this surging tide, a willing castaway
On a welcome beach of fern and flower,
I laze, a happy beachcomber, in wanton idleness,
And while away a carefree seashore hour.

AUGUST EVENING

Far away across the patchwork fields
A wistful, dulcet, gently tolling bell
Once more called a faithful few to prayer,
As evening's gathering shadows softly fell

To blend and deepen, imperceptibly,
And hypnotise my spellbound watching eye,
Held captive by the ever-changing light
On woodland, pasture, meadow, stream and sky.

A magic limning haze suffused the whole
With afterglow's enchanting conjuring,
Whilst rimming the surrounding darkling hills,
Corona-like, in smouldered shimmering.

The softened fading flares of setting sun
Sent mellow molten beams through woodland's edge
And, lace-like, trimmed the towering drowsing oaks
With hems of glinting golden foliage,

Whilst burnishing the soughing meadow grass
With swaying sequin sparks of dancing light –
A restless iridescent play of fire
That caused my dazzled eye bemused delight.

The rippling tide-like fields of ripened grain
Troughed and swelled and troughed like ochre seas,
Whilst blood-red poppies rode each surging crest
Like blithe vermilion sea anemones.

Enfolding dusk drew ever close about,
As flitting bats explored the dimming skies,
And barn owls roused from their diurnal rest
To scan the scene with predatory eyes.

And other creatures, shyly shunning day,
Resumed their furtive nocturnal affairs
And lay in wait for their unwary prey,
With tooth and claw and deadly web and snare.

I heard and sensed their stirrings all around
As ever-deepening dusk enveloped all,
And shadowed prey and hunter pitted wits –
Some to survive, the luckless ones to fall.

A crescent moon stole coyly up the sky
To silver everything that had been gold.
A night breeze whispered softly on my skin;
I shivered – from enchantment, not from cold.

And homeward then I strolled through leaf-lined lanes,
My mind stirred by the beauty of it all.
Such calm contentment filled my solitude,
Whilst relishing that wonderful nightfall.

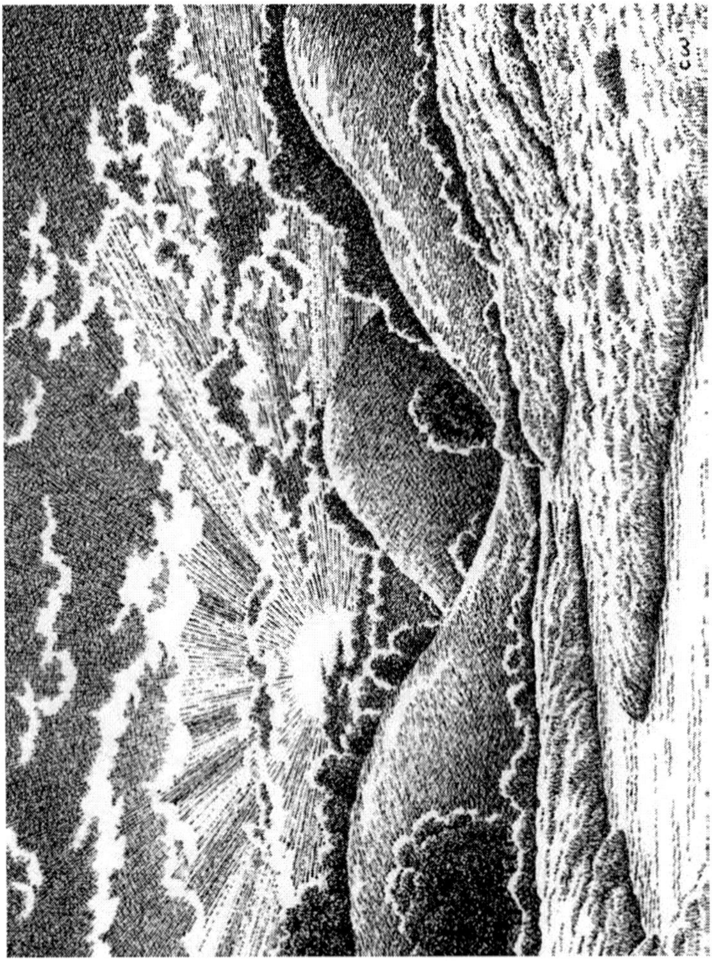

SUMMER SUNSET

As the sun slowly sank down the shimmering sky
And melted the evening away,
And hung, as if gilding the edge of the world,
While bidding farewell to the day;

For a time every tree on the hill seemed on fire,
And molten gold flowed in the stream,
And shadows grew longer and deeper before
The flare of that last dying gleam.

For a long dreamlike moment I gazed, held in awe,
As the sun seemed to hang, hesitating,
Transfixed by the beauty of all that I saw,
And reluctant to yield to night's waiting.

Still I lingered, enjoying that slow-fading glow,
As the gentlest of night breezes stirred,
While the chirrup of crickets replaced late birdsong,
And a foraging owl could be heard.

Then I turned, crossed the field and climbed over the stile,
And then down the darkening lane
I wandered, beguiled by the loveliness
And wonder of nature again.

A SUMMER GLADE

Idling, solitary in a fern-rimmed, drowsing glade
In summer sun-steeped mellow mote-swirled light,
Through the dazzling sunspill darts and swaying dapple shade,
I watched a magpie's brash and gaudy flight.

Through shifting tiger stripes of shadow lanced by flaring gleams,
With startling harsh staccato rattle-call,
The brazen piebald terror screeched its strident rasping screams,
Then cackled out of sight, and silence fell.

Beneath an ancient ivied oak with fibrositic boughs,
A ghost of wizened glory, gnarled by age,
I stepped between great spreading roots through comfrey and wild rose,
And pale green, gold-flecked drifts of saxifrage.

Close by the glade, between mossed banks, and fringed by sedge and reeds,
With unobtrusive chuckling melody,
A glinting brook wound through the trees, with no apparent need
For haste, or any sense of where to be.

Where tangled flotsam checked the flow, a slender willow leaned
To trail spread fingers in the tiny weir,
And, through the ripples, shimmer-sparks of darting minnows gleamed,
While scented chanterelle spores tinged the air.

Above, the sun might sear the leaves, but here in dappled cool,
At ease in perfect peace in greenswathe shade,
I lingered, lulled by cricket buzz and distant redstarts' calls,
And wanted no more than that summer glade.

THE HARVEST

The gentle morning spread itself across the rolling fields,
And dew-cooled air breathed freshness through the ripened ochre grain.
Old Thomas led the plodding shires along the track and past the byre
To harvester and hay cart waiting down by Malthouse Lane.

The brambles twining through the hedgerows sagged with swollen fruit,
A treasure trove for bird and insect, harvest mouse and vole –
And village children, fingertips the colour of their juice-stained lips,
who'd cram their eager mouths to bursting on their way to school.

Harnessed up, the horses answered Tom's command to pull
And, clackingly, the combine's wooden blades began to cleave.
The tied sheaves dropped out one by one, were neatly stooked* by Tom's young son
who, kerchief round his face and grey with dust, could barely breathe.

From high up on the Ridgeway, with its crown of coppiced beech,
The combine's clatter muted to a gently clacking beat,
The man, the youth and horses looked like figures in a picture book
As back and forth and row by row they felled the golden wheat.

Within the yet remaining crop the rhythmic clatter grew
And, to the tenants' dread, their peaceful haven was no more,
And countless field mice fled in fright the wooden blades' approaching bite;
The seasons' turning meant the end of summer at their door.

By evening all the stooks* were serried round the stubbled field,
Like sentinels drawn up to guard the gleanings in the dust.
Old Thomas paused, surveyed the scene, then wiped his brow, unhitched the team;
The harvest was complete, the weary shires led home to rest.

*stook – sheaves of wheat or other cereal stacked together to dry in bygone days

AUTUMN PASTORAL

The genteel charms of autumn trailed their fraying hems in dews,
As languorously briefer grew the mellow dwindling days,
And mist wraiths hugged the riverbank till breeze-breaths teased them free,
While distant fields and tree-gowned hills were filmed with smoke-blue haze.

And, bluer still, the far horizon fused the earth to air,
Confusing where the one might end, and where the other start,
A wavering and melting border merging land and sky,
As if the two were undecided how to be apart.

Below the Downs the village clustered round its church and green,
Where winding lane and river had a meeting of the ways
And, bordered by their hedges and their sun-warmed lichened walls,
The patchwork fields and paddocks ambled down in jigsaw maze.

The stubbled fields, a playground now for partridges and hares,
Glowed richly ochre-gold beneath the warm September skies.
The orchards' few remaining unpicked fruits drew insect life –
Red admirals and tortoiseshells, bees, wasps and hover flies.

Beside a hedge, in drying hay, a sunning fox snatched sleep,
One eye half open, still alert, eyes pricked for any sound
And, while he dozed, the field mice safely scurried through the hedge,
And wary rooks, dark gleaners, picked such spoils as might be found.

At river's edge, below the mill and just beyond its race,
A water vole crouched nibbling in a twist of tangled reeds,
Then with a tail-twitch swam to shore and climbed the burrowed bank
And shook himself till water droplets flew like crystal beads.

Downstream the water meadow sparkled, lush and rich with life,
And moorhens, water rails and herons scanned its fertile edge,
And plump contented cattle grazed on sweet grass and kingcups,
And iridescent mallards foraged through the reeds and sedge.

The peaceful village, lane and stream lay basking in the haze;
The sleepy fox yawned, stretched and scratched, then yawned and dozed again.
The little valley nestled in its flanking beech-crowned hills,
Untroubled by the world beyond its pastoral domain.

HIATUS

A sense of pensive waiting, a diffident hiatus;
Autumn paused, almost as in suspension, meditation.

Swallows, swifts and martins fled the dwindling daylight hours,
Drawn south in arrow flights to where drab winter has no power.
One wonders just how few these lovely mist filled mornings yet
Will wistful lingering mellow sun-warmed tranquil days beget.

Berries crammed with juice that fill the hedgerows, vines and bushes
Lining lanes where once cow parsley soared in lacy masses,
And drifts of sweetest cicely romped, cloudlike, with vervain
Predict a bitter winter, if there's truth in that old saying.

Even now the hardy dog rose keeps some fragile blooms,
While fattened caterpillars metamorphose in cocoons,
With larders of field mice and squirrels partially laid in;
And yet there are still ox-eye daisies, hawkbit, gentian.

No frost as yet, though dawn chill takes more time each day to warm,
And winter waits within the wings, impatient to perform,
And daily briefer grow the hours when sunlight still holds sway.
Just how much longer can they last – these soft hiatus days?

THE END OF AUTUMN

How like a well-loved fading actor
Graceful autumn leaves her stage –
By stages.

Bit parts linger now and then,
Walk-ons recalling golden days
Between the greys.

Short skits and sketches soon are all
Remaining, till her final role's
Last curtain fall.

The wistful audience must now
Attend another opening show
And winter's mocking bow.

THE VILLAGE IN AUTUMN

The razor-keen morning nipped noses and fingertips,
Frost-sparked the thorns on the old bramble hedge,
Crystalled the telephone wires with ice baubles
And sequinned the leaf drifts along the lane's edge.

The bared ribs of ploughed earth lay waiting and empty,
Except for the bleak crop of furrow-turned flints.
From Merryworth Lane to the yew-shaded churchyard
The hop poles reached up like a forest of splints.

The pewter-skied morning soon turned to pale silver
And warmed the lulled landscape and foraging crows.
The telephone wires shed their ice pearls like teardrops;
The sleepy-eyed village shook off its repose.

Old Tom brushed the shires and fed each one an apple,
Then fitted the harness and hitched up the cart
And rubbed calloused hands till the blood sang within them,
All set for another day's labour to start.

The cracked school bell cackled its termagant jangle;
The children assembled in chilled, jostling bands
And pushed and punched playfully all through the roll call,
And wiped away dewdrops with backs of red hands.

The plans were afoot for next week's harvest festival,
Rector and WI ladies to meet
At two o'clock sharp in the Methodist church hall
Behind the pub car park in Latimer Street.

Old Mrs Simpson's congested emporium
Doggedly fought the temptations of town,
Her Post Office counter the village's centre,
Though faceless accountants might want it closed down.

The day ambled by with the business of village life,
Jennifer's Tea Room quite busy by four,
While windows of baker and butcher were emptying;
Soon the closed signs would be turned on each door.

School was out; scampering kids made their homeward way,
Cottage lights flickered on, welcoming, warm.
Fires were lit, kitchen aromas were beckoning;
Tom led the shires down the track to the barn.

A blue tinge of wood smoke hung over the beech wood,
And Gipsy John's log cart creaked under its load,
As he trundled it noisily over the cobbles
For folk to stock up before winter took hold.

The day's end dissolved in the hazing of twilight,
As diffident evening stole on to the scene.
The sun set unhurriedly, veining the dimming sky,
Drawing behind it the dusk, like a screen.

Rooks flew to roost with their night-herald chorusing,
Leaving late rabbits to quarter the fields.
The village in autumn had reached one more close of day,
Snug in the gathering folds of the Weald.

COMING HOME

Life's summer had mellowed to soft, dwindling days,
And each saw an image grow ever more clear,
Till autumn's spell drew me with such urgent charm,
That the call of my village was all I could hear.

I'd often been back down the unwinding years,
Drawn by nostalgia for sights, sounds and scents,
And those left behind, whittled fewer by time,
But, lately, the leaving had been more intense.

The lane's twists and turns, enigmatic these days,
Had once bounded small fields, dictating its course
Before fields were merged and their hedges grubbed out,
When speed was the pace of a hay cart and horse.

The dog rose-decked blackthorn that borders the lane
And marks where its way had wound since ancient days,
A home still for hedgehog and dunnock and vole,
Survives, unlike much of its kind, long since razed.

The cobbles are worn on the steep village street,
Polished by iron rims of wheels of past days.
The quaint huddled cottages lean like old men
Too tired to fall down, or too set in their ways.

I'd been away too long, it seemed to me now,
And ached to be part of the village again,
To lean like an old man too tired to fall down,
And spend my last years in the place I began.

THE STRIPPER

As, unashamed, she sheds her clothes,
Rude Autumn mimics Gypsy Rose,
Strips her raiments, unabashed,
And casts them off like tarty trash.
Litters woodland, lane and field
And flaunts, her nakedness revealed.
Brazen hussy – she's so bold –
But later . . . brrrr, she'll feel the cold!

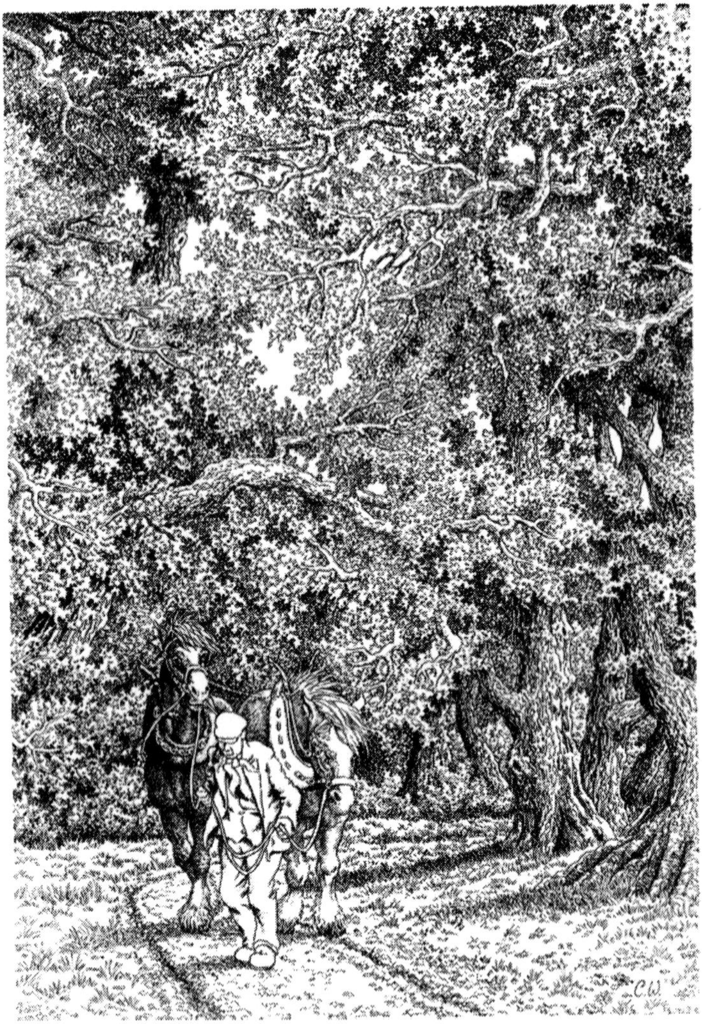

THE TEAM

Dawn is sheen of mother-of-pearl,
With dew globe glint on fresh-turned hay.
Snorted clouds of warm breath-mist
Hang, wraith-like, round each horse's head
As, up the track with massive tread,
The mighty shires begin their day.

Wheat stalks crunching underfoot,
Old Jonsy leads them to the plough,
And soon the share bites deep and sure,
Baring field's flesh to the light
And opportunist crows' delight,
As Jonsy wipes his wind-burned brow.

One by one the furrows form,
As turn and turn again are made,
With lines as straight as arrow flight.
No trace remains of stubble gleam
As homeward trudge the mighty team,
The day's work done, at rest the blade.

SUMMERGONE

Though dog rose blooms still grace the hedge-lined leas,
And tireless ever-optimistic bees
Toil ceaselessly from vetch to saxifrage,
The spinning seasons turn yet one more page.

Now dawn's dew film precedes each golden haze,
And fewer are the hours that warm the days,
While afternoons that once lazed long and slow
Speed by to dusk and mistier moon-glow.

With susurrating breath, the autumn breeze
Soughs gently through the woodland's rustling leaves,
Confiding tales it brings from south and west,
Then moving on with restless wanderlust

To north and east, its journey not complete,
Across the pastures and the fields of wheat.
Murmuring all the while, it bends to yield
Its traveller's tales to hedge and brook and field.

To lake and river too it whispers low
Of where it's been and where it's still to go,
Till, with one last farewell, it passes on,
Leaving just the echo of its song.

AUTUMN'S END

Skies of breeze-blown gossamer,
Sweet ripe juice of hip and haw,
Morning mist, then golden haze
Enhance the spell of autumn days.

Dew clings late to gate and hedge
And, with each dawn, a crisper edge
Reminds us, briskly, summer's gone,
And north wind's bite is soon to come.

Leaves turn gold, red, russet, brown
In vivid splendour – autumn's crown.
They flaunt and dazzle, court the eye,
Then, wind-thieved, wither, fall and die.

Distant now the heat of days
When leaves umbrellaed blazing rays
As, idling through some woodland glade,
We sheltered in their welcome shade.

Gone now summer's memoried heat –
In fruitful hedges berried deep.
These dwindling days of dreaming fall
Now predict old winter's call.

In mellow light the sighing breeze
Strips woodlands of their parchment leaves,
Their once luxuriant canopies
Soon drifts of fading memories.

Then glinting sunlight flickers play
On naked branches' wistful sway
In breezes chilled by autumn's end,
Till springtime sees them green again.

LAMPLIGHT AT SUPPER TIME

Days of winds of arctic howling,
Nights of Jack Frost's icy prowling;
Snowdrifts blocking lanes and byways
Severed villages from highways.
In that winter how we, nightly
By the log fire, huddled tightly,
While the knife-wind's frenzied clamour
Struck our windows like a hammer.
In the fitful candle-flutter –
Leaping, waning, wax a-gutter –
Fringes of the drowsing darkness,
Corners lost in dim remoteness,
Stirred like half-forgotten legends
Slumbering in shadowed regions.
Shifting shapes, they slyly woke
In draught-swirled eddies of sweet smoke.
Dipping, dancing, stretching, flinching;
Monsters looming, towering, shrinking
Fuelled our imaginations
With such conjuring gyrations.
Dragons, unicorns, chimeras
Filled our minds with friendly terrors.
Ogres leapt, not quite unbidden,
Coaxed from shadows where they'd hidden.
Then a bustling from the kitchen
Spoke of supper, mother pitching
Sweet digestives on a platter,
Cocoa smells, teaspoons a-clatter.
Lamps were lit and candles dimmed,
And cocoa sipped before it skinned.
In the lamplight monsters fled,
So – up the 'wooden hill' to bed!

FROSTY MORNING

Bleak dawn bites sharp, blue-veined, flesh-numbing raw-
A splintered, snapping snatch-breath, brittling bones
And razor-blading at my fingertips,
As I scrape ice-crepe patterns from the panes.

The frost-glaze glitter splinters at my eyes,
Sliver-slicing, scythe-like through their squint.
I raise my ice-numbed flinching hands to shield
My blinded glance from lancing, white-light glint,

Then scuttle to the rug from floorboard-freeze,
Haul huffed-in socks on cringing, bloodless feet,
And puff a trail of breath-mist in my wake,
My slipper-scuffing scurry to the street.

The jagged air stabs lung deep as I stoop
To prise the bottle from step's spangled clasp.
A silver-topped ice mushroom stops the neck;
Frost-crystalled glass welds to my shrinking grasp.

From stove-warmed kitchen, sipping tea, I gaze
As dawn-blaze silver slowly melts away
In coruscating gems of tinsel frost,
Sequinning this crisp midwinter day.

IN WILDWOOD WINTER

The brook, beneath its icy mask,
Made strangled gaspings in its frozen throat,
Like one with skin stretched parchment-tight across old bone.
Raw winter closely clenched his savage vicy grasp
And pierced his vicious thorn through thickest hide and coat
Of all within that wildwood night, as bitter north wind sliced,
And barbed frost thrust his blade in helpless tree and stone.

Claw-like against the howling sky,
Stark talons of skeletal branches raked
In manic wind-whipped uncontrolled convulsion.
And while the night's ill temper raged its lunacy,
A hundred pulses skipped and quickened, faint hearts quaked
In labryinthine fastnesses mazed deep through tangled roots
In crouching dread in wildwood's gale-beset confusion.

In panic's grip at every squall,
Transfixed were all in burrow, den and lair.
Resigned to winter's arctic blast, breath-stilled they lay.
The badger, rabbit, fox, frail tiny shrew and all
The wildwood's hapless huddled creatures, foul and fair,
From bravest heart to timidest of cowering, wretched wreck
Stayed, spellbound as the frenzied, freezing night held sway.

But pale dawn calmed the frantic storm
And, with the sudden hush, the faintest sound
Of muffled pattering sighed through that wildwood bare,
And, magically, snow's gentle tranquil mantling form
Bewitched bewildered waking wildwood all around,
Transformed familiar features to a white-clad wonderland,
As cautious creatures stirred into a changed world there.

And, one by one, they ventured out
With wary glare-flinch gaze and steamy breath,
And trailed their wonder through the drifts of silentness.
For that one frozen disconnect of time no snout
Sought out, for once, the vital scents of life or death,
Or yet begrudged its neighbour space or time to marvel there,
Or knew the thought of bloodlust in that wilderness.

SNOW

Snow –bleak winter's ticker-tape salute –
A strangely comforting white overcoat
Makes my neglected garden no more plain
Than better manicured ones in the lane.

With shrouded rust and registration plate,
My car's as nice as all of later date,
And flaking windowsills in need of paint
Are picturesque and Christmas cardy quaint.

My untrimmed privet hedge, so long my shame,
Hides slumbering beneath snow's counterpane,
And broken slates disfiguring my roof –
Now covered – can no longer draw reproof.

I like snow's kind disguise; long may it last,
Whilst hiding un-dug weeds and uncut grass,
And aged vehicle, incognito.

Don't like the winter, but I love its snow!

A COTSWOLD FARMHOUSE WINTER

How the frozen land creaked, aching,
Bitten to the marrow of its bones;
Jet-dark, the ice-bound night, flint-edged the wind,
While the snow-encrusted earth
Wheezed in its cold-congested throat
And gasped its hoary breath from lungs frost-rimed.

All around, the deep of midnight
Cloaked the land and pressed against the door,
And north wind howled its rage in frenzied moil,
And frost stole into every crack
And skeined the glass – without, within –
And burned our chilblained toes as blood recoiled.

We huddled by the kitchen range
And stifled yawns, pretending still
The hour was not so late – not bedtime yet.
But when, too soon, the embers dimmed,
And candles guttered fitfully,
The stygian stairwell gaped its arctic threat.

Then glacial sheets as stiff as boards
Were tormentors of flinching flesh
Forced down their chill crevasse while teeth were clenched,
And coward blood fled out of toes,
While fingers felt for armpit warmth,
Until the body's heat returned at length.

And then the razor-bladed wind
Could screech for all its furied worth
And hurl its wrath against our window panes,
Whilst we, now snugly blanketed,
Unlocked our limbs, succumbed to sleep
Till morning, and the kitchen range again.

MIDWINTER NIGHT

Arctic night stalks through the village,
Fangs bared in a frozen kiss,
Savagely unsheathing talons,
Glittering and merciless.

Razor chill pervades each cottage
With its manacle embrace.
Tentacles of brittle shivers
Haunt each dark unheated space.

Bedtime, and reluctant young ones
Climb the dim ice-box stairwell,
From the kitchen's haven glow
To the bedroom's polar chill.

Bare feet flinch on freezing floorboards,
Scurry to the bedside rugs,
Inch down stiff sheets' glacial challenge;
Arms clutch knees in wretched hugs.

Breath-mist icing veins the windows,
Bloodless toes feel chilblains burn;
Feet that find hot-water bottles
Throb with pain as blood returns.

Moonlight filters through the jigsaw
Ice-shards patterning the panes,
Paints a pale kaleidoscope
About the walls in lacy skeins.

Locked in frost, the land creaks quietly,
Deep-pierced by the ice-thorned air;
Snapping silence shrinks and crackles,
Pinned beneath the moon's bleak stare.

Night is jewel-bright, turned crystal –
Petrified, locked tight and sealed.
Freezing vapour rimes the woodland,
Pearls the hedgerows, lanes and fields.

Catch-breath night cows down, defenceless,
Rib-white in ice kingdom's grasp,
Hoar-confectioned, stilled and waiting,
Sighing one long frozen gasp.

HERDWICK EWES IN FEBRUARY

As winter hugs its perished flanks
And wraps its ribs with thick snowflesh,
The storm-lashed, steam-breathed upland sheep
Crowd for comfort, closely pressed –

Weather-bunched and huddle-hunching
Hard against the dry stone wall,
Fleeces caked with sleet-wind dressing,
Wretchedly resigned to all.

Hooves paw vainly at the white mask
Of the snow-scabbed, ice-veined fell;
Pasture now held in a vice-clasp,
Locked beneath the frost's iron shell.

Herdwick ewes in February
Flinch beneath a howling sky,
Suffer nature's harshest trials
To lamb in spring as north winds die.

OUR VILLAGE – NOVEMBER 1917
(A childhood memory)

The dead man came by night sometimes; we'd hear his dragging step,
But never when bright moonlight filled the moor.
The rusty hinges of the gate would sound, and then we'd hear
A muffled tapping at the kitchen door.

The door would open gently, and we'd tiptoe to the stairs,
Our nightshirts gathered round us, Jack and I.
We'd eavesdrop as our mother's voice would utter gentle words,
And sometimes we would hear the dead man cry.

We knew our mother fed him with what little could be spared –
A bowl of boiled bone soup, a crust of bread.
The smell of him would creep up to the landing where we'd crouch:
Wet moorland, unwashed greatcoat, sweat and dread.

The war's third year was near its end, and fewer were the few
Who came back to their homes for leave's brief spell,
And dead-eyed men would mutter quietly of the waste of war,
Or slump in silence, staring into hell.

One day police and soldiers came and scoured the brooding moor;
We knew the dead man would not call again.
While neighbours spoke of justice for deserters' cowardice,
Our mother wept for souls of broken men.

They said a crust of mouldy bread lay in his tight-closed hand,
A piece more, quite un-chewed, was in his mouth,
As if to chew, to swallow, was too much to contemplate,
The will to live now spent with his lost youth.

OLD WINTER

The spiteful northerly-bred winds
Hurled winter's needle-pointed frosted barbs
That seared the eyes and bruised the skin,
And cowed and bent, with fusillading shards
Of crystalled ice, each mortal, frail,
Who dared to brave the stinging hail.

In slip-slide staggers, limbs awry,
On cautious feet, with stiff-legged puppet steps,
A few intrepid souls passed by,
And each – on firm ground steady – seemed inept,
Like toddlers learning how to stand,
Counterbalancing with outstretched hands.

Clad in longjohns, fleeces, scarves,
Cocooned in layered sweaters, overcoats,
We carapaced our fear with laughs
And tiptoed our bravado down the slopes,
And eyed the young ones on their sleds
And prayed we wouldn't fall and break our heads.

Underfoot, the ice coat brittly cracked
And snapped its malice at our timid heels,
And all we oldies coughed and wheezed and hacked,
As frost-tipped spicules hurtled – tracer shells –
Into our frozen faces, chilled
By more than just the thought of being old.

THE DREAMER

By a bend in a lane at the edge of a wood,
Where a meadow slopes down in an unhurried way
To a moss-shouldered brook with its low chuckling song
That lazily winds and meanders along,
And in mellow sun-shafts darting damselflies play,
While the gentlest of breezes makes willow fronds sway,
You may find a dreamer leant back on a tree.
Just leave him daydreaming; it's probably me.

How Very English – Some Reviews

'Sheer poetic genius!' (*his mother*)

'Shakespeare, he ain't' (*his English teacher*)

'To be honest, I've always thought poetry's a bit cissyfied. Seems like a nice enough bloke, though' (*a neighbour*)

'Poetry, my ass!' (*Harry Callahan*)